EXTREME HEROISM

EXTREME HEROISM

Rev. Dr. John Prochaska

EXTREME HEROISM

iUniverse books may be ordered through booksellers or by contacting:

iUniverse
1663 Liberty Drive
Bloomington, IN 47403
www.iuniverse.com
1-800-Authors (1-800-288-4677)

ISBN: 978-1-5320-0194-9 (sc)
ISBN: 978-1-5320-0195-6 (e)

Library of Congress Control Number: 2016911195

Print information available on the last page.

iUniverse rev. date: 09/15/2016

THE AUTHOR

Ordained in 1976, Eugene J. (John) Prochaska is now retired from professional ministry, living in Canada. He has enjoyed full standing in three denominations: The United Church of Canada, The United Church of Christ and The Christian Church (Disciples of Christ). He has served over twenty church institutions in Canada (Alberta and British Columbia) and the United States (Washington, Texas, Nebraska and Wyoming).

In seminary he immersed in advanced pastoral counseling and the Jungian school of psychotherapy. While still in seminary he studied with the Wholistic Cancer Treatment Institute in Ft. Worth, Texas. He later served as counselor and director of community services for the Pastoral Institute of Calgary, Alberta. He was awarded a Master of Divinity degree in 1976 and a Doctor of Ministry degree in 1981 from Brite Divinity School, Texas Christian University, Ft. Worth, Texas.

Prior to his life as a clergyman, John was 3 years with the U.S. Army in South Korea and then the petroleum industry for almost 20 years in Wyoming, Montana, Texas, Colorado and Alberta, Canada. He received a degree in petroleum engineering in 1956 from Casper College, Casper, Wyoming; a Bachelor of Science degree in 1959 and a Master of Arts in geology in 1960 from the University of Wyoming. John has written as a geologist, a micro-paleontologist and as a parish minister. In seminary he studied New Testament Greek and applied it seriously for over 30 years as a parish minister in day-to-day biblical interpretation for weekly preaching and daily ministry which led to his insights into heroism.

CONTENTS

SECTION II

EXTREME HEROISM: AN ARRAY OF APPROPRIATE RESPONSES TO INJUSTICE

SECTION III

OBSTACLES, RESTRAINTS, DISCOURAGEMENTS TO EXTREME HEROISM

SECTION IV

EXTREME HEROISM: THE WHOLE THING

PREFACE

Heroism. This book is about heroism and specifically, a kind of heroism which I have called extreme...extreme heroism. The rationale for defining parts of heroism as extreme but not others, is in itself an intriguing study.

While looking closely at extreme heroism as a lifestyle, the book also focuses on heroism as a language by which every society finds a way to speak of their realities in being human. While the book frequently borrows illustrations from the languages of religion and spirituality, the two are not meant to be the primary focus. Since this will be the first time for many to think of heroism as a language, know that it may be the only language available to vast numbers of people not conversant with religion or spirituality.

Obviously, the language of extreme heroism as such, is a sublanguage within English. It is comparable to the sublanguages spoken by medical professionals to each other or by experts to other experts in say astrophysics, theology, chemistry, computer science, religion, spirituality, psychology, psychiatry, etc. However, unlike these high profile sub-languages, the language of heroism is more a language of the street, but that should not be cause for discrediting.

It is an informal language not taught in classrooms but rather by personal experience and by peers. It is the language of the hallway between classes, the language of the playground, the language of the locker room, the language of the curling rink, the bowling alley or the parking lot…the language of all the informal places in society where we see one another at our worst and best. Once learned, this informal language never leaves us, but for some it does get set aside where it remains rudimentary as we age and substitute the formal languages learned in classroom and laboratory.

It is said of the times in which we now live that a significantly large percentage of people no longer speak the formal language of religion or spirituality, so they resort to other sublanguages like the ones abiding in our memories. Those steeped in the language of religion and spirituality would do well to remember the many who have no language for talking about important life issues. This book would cater to those without a formal language and those who care about conversing with them.

While languages sometimes create unnecessary division between nations and tribes, there are things about being human that do not change and those include our inclination to do heroic things from time to time. Heroism can be intentional but more often it is random. Fortunately for everyone the language of extreme heroism is simple and easy to learn and develop at every age. There are just a few rules to remember as we respond to the multitude of opportunities coming our way every day for producing a just, meaningful and joyful world through extreme heroism.

PROLOGUE

Language of Heroism

Paul Archambault had been judged a criminal by the provincial court of Alberta (Shaben 2012), but on a flight taking him to conviction and sentencing, his true heroic nature emerged. He responded to an injustice and did *the right thing.*

To the media it appeared he had done something abnormal, but to Paul it felt normal. They called it heroism, but Paul resisted for a time before accepting that saving the lives of 3 others including his RCMP escort was both normal and heroic.

Language of Religion

In the following we hear an ancient writer striving to describe something priceless, precious and the best of human behavior through words that would later appear at the heart of a major world religion.

"What has come into being in him was life and the life was the light of all people. "Sixteen verses later these words are given a human name - Jesus. (John 1:3b-4) (Holy Bible, The New Revised Standard Version 1997)

Language of Spirituality

"Our deepest fear is not that we are inadequate. Our deepest fear is that we are powerful beyond measure. It is our *light,* not our darkness that most frightens us. Actually, who are you not to be? You are a child of God."

"Your playing-small does not serve the world. There is nothing enlightened about shrinking so that other people won't feel insecure around you. We are all meant to shine, as children do. We were born to make manifest the glory of God that is within us." (Williamson 1992).

An Unplanned Meeting with the Indwelling Hero

Late one bitterly cold winter night in October, 1984, during a fast-moving snow storm barreling south across Alberta, Canada, a commuter airliner carrying 10 people went down in a rugged area near the northern city of Grande Prairie. The crash killed six. The four who survived, according to author Carol Shaben (Shaben 2012), were the pilot, an Alberta Cabinet Minister (Carol's father), a Royal Canadian Mounted Police officer and his prisoner, Paul Archambault.

Paul Archambault was being escorted north to face criminal charges in a provincial court but for the moment he was about to become a survivor of a plane crash with people lying dead or gravely injured around him and he was about to meet his indwelling extreme hero. He would surprise himself and others by taking responsibility for the survivors. For several hours Paul would repeatedly exercise extreme heroism for three others which is more commonly known on the street as *doing the right thing*.

Through a fortuitous earlier decision by his RCMP escort* to remove Paul's handcuffs in flight, he was free after the crash to do pretty much as he pleased. Being as free of injury as he was he could have left the crash site seeking to disappear into the wilderness where he was comfortable…or stay and help survivors. He could have left his RCMP escort buried and suffocating beneath the twisted wreckage, or dig him out, drag him a safe distance away and start a fire that would provide warmth for the four of them. Because he was the only one able, Paul was free to do the minimal work required for finding more firewood beneath the snow and to keep the fire going for everyone…or not. He could watch his RCMP escort die OR tend to his wounds; find blankets in the plane to keep him and the others warm until rescuers arrived… or not. Paul acted heroically, choosing all the right things which kept the other three alive until a search-and-rescue party reached the crash site and evacuated everyone to a regional hospital.

It wasn't long after their reaching Edmonton that individual accounts of what happened began to emerge from interviews with the four. All three of the other survivors agreed that Paul had saved their lives and two even used the word *hero*. News reporters covering the crash were quick to recognize that this was going to be a fascinating story of credible and somehow, the real deal, in terms of a heroism that everyone could agree was heroic.

What few would be aware of as the news media laid the mantle of hero onto Paul's shoulders, that they would set in motion three predictable phases that were made predictable by a strange love/hate relationship which many English-speaking people have with the concept of heroism: (1) Paul's rejection of the title, (2) his tentative acceptance of the title followed by ascendance to a new way of thinking about himself, and then (3) a falling back to old ways of thinking, being and doing. As if on cue, Paul quickly entered phase one, rejecting any notion that he was a hero – like combat soldiers do when told they are going to be honored by their nation for bravery and valor.

Phase two is what happens when there has been persistent hero-talk by friends, media representatives or even one persistent individual. If this phase lasts long enough the recipient will soften his/her resistance and begin to accept that maybe there is some truth to what everyone is saying and that he might be a little bit deserving of the name hero after all. As newly christened heroes become more and more comfortable with this new thinking they begin behaving differently.

In Paul's case there was extra reinforcement from a provincial judge who reviewed the charges against Paul after a full accounting of his behavior in the plane crash. The criminal charges that had been pending were dropped and Paul was set free. He returned to his friends as a hero, not a criminal or bum or a loser…which is one incarnation of the third phase as newly recognized heroes either return to their former social networks and support systems, or they move on to new ones.

Heroes born of a supportive social network, whose friends remain supportive after acknowledging and applauding a hero in their midst, are likely to move on up in their own estimation as well as the eyes of their support system. They are likely then to live more courageous and confident lives.

Networks of the opposite nature often enjoy the glow from their very own hero for a brief time but soon lose interest. The kind of support needed by newly discovered heroes for establishing a new baseline of behavior, may dissipate without it. Newly morphed heroes can morph in the opposite direction back to the way things used to be which is tragic…because it doesn't have to be this way.

Health and Psychology writer, Ginny Graves, writing about trauma survivors in general, mentions a relatively new behavioral term called Post Traumatic Growth or PTG. While many know about PTSD or Post-Traumatic Stress Disorder (PTSD) and the way it puts lives on hold, there may be more to be said in time about PTG which refers to remarkable changes in a survivor's desire to make the world a better place. In a recent magazine article, Ginny asks rhetorically: "*Is There an Upside to Tragedy*?" (Graves 2015). The answer given is 'Yes" as she refers to trauma survivors making and sustaining significant changes in their post-traumatic behavior. If some trauma survivors can do more than survive, perhaps all trauma survivors can.

Tragically, Paul Archambault, a recognized hero, would be found by authorities seven years later, all alone, frozen to death, buried beneath another winter snow not far from the crash site where his indwelling hero first emerged. We know he was loved, supported, admired and affirmed, but it's unclear why that wasn't enough.

After the indwelling hero emerges it seems that some people, maybe most, need something resembling a 'midwife' to watch over them, teach them and guide them like a child until they have secured for themselves a new baseline of behavior. Newly born heroes can truly be compared to new-born infants who need immediate and sustained attention until they are able to walk through life in a new way. Unfortunately our societies are not well structured for providing that guidance.

All U.S. Congressional Medal of Honor recipients in the past 7 years have had similar reactions to being named heroes, insisting correctly that they are no more deserving than the ones whose lives they saved. "I only did what I had to do." and "I only did what I was trained to do."

Perhaps another way of saying it is that everyone bears within them the inclination of an indwelling extreme hero. Like other heroes, most heroes given national recognition are heroes who need as much persuasion as anyone else to accept the accolades of their country. Commanders and others in authority, even the President of the United States or the Prime Minister of Canada are sometimes called upon to persuade a nominee by consoling themselves with the idea that: "While it's true that the heroic impulse resides in everyone, your comrades and you, even so you must accept this recognition on their behalf."

In order that this book be usable as a teaching tool, there is at the conclusion of each story/illustration an analysis which identifies (1) injustice motivating the hero to act and (2) evidence that responses were guided by indiscourageable good will for all involved. For example: **(1) What is more unjust than a plane crash with people dead or dying? (2) Paul's response included his RCMP escort. Hardened criminals might have been reluctant to assist a police officer. Paul helped all the survivors, including his handler and even himself in the process.**

A Love-Hate Relationship with Heroism

Most days when the television talk show "*Jimmy Kimmel Live*" (ABC) is being taped at its theatre location in Los Angeles, California, several individuals can be seen outside on Hollywood Boulevard dressed in various super-hero costumes...Captain America, Spiderman, Superman, Super Woman, Iron Man, Wonder Woman and others. These iconic characters have become unofficial fixtures of the show. Visitors passing by might naturally conclude from this faithful display that Americans put a high value on heroism. Obviously there are some Americans who do, but there is a lot of anecdotal evidence to suggest otherwise.

Television viewers in Canada and the United States, beginning with the Fall Season of 2015, found themselves presented with two new prime-time hero shows to choose from for entertainment: CBS's offering of "*Supergirl*" and NBC's offering of "*Heroes Reborn*". More hero-based programs are promised before the year is over and again, it might be concluded from this that North Americans are really "into" the concept of heroism...at least the television industry thinks so.

If we concede that there is a certain level of interest in heroism out there then we have to wonder where it's coming from; from what parts of Canadian and U.S. societies? Why are so few pleased then to be hailed as a hero? Why is heroism not more a part of our national conversation? This contradiction among English-speaking people is one of the things that started me down the path toward writing a book that would eventually be called *Extreme Heroism.*

When asked to define the word hero most people have a reasonably sound idea about its meaning. Former War Correspondent (WWII) and CBS news commentator, the late Andy Rooney, described it the way most people like to hear it: "Being a hero means doing something that risks your own life while you're saving someone else's." (Rooney 2009). People seem to have a soft spot in their heart for heroism defined that way and freely admit to admiring those who take risks for the good of others, yet do they feel all warm and fuzzy about the word applied to them? Not so much and that seems very, very odd; it's like a saintly Christian not owning up to their own saintly acts, or a self-identified spiritualist denying their own gentleness, kindness and joyfulness.

In my experience colored by 40 years as a clergyman, 20 years as a science professional, 11 years as a university student and 3 years in the military, heroism has become conspicuous by its absence from public discourse. The word is bandied about, but without much definition. Heroism sometimes seems like one of the great non-issues of our time, even among English-speaking Christians who exhibit the most vigorous resistance to being associated with heroism, even though encouraged to think of themselves as saintly members of a holy priesthood. Where then does this attitude toward heroism come from?

From my life among Christians since the teen years, I can't say I've ever heard a sermon condemning heroism nor have I ever sat in a Church school class or a seminary class where heroism was defined and then denounced. I have never seen or heard a directive to Christians telling them not to use the word hero and yet we seem to obey some unwritten, unspoken rule against even friendly association with the word. Just recently I came across an article by a professional minister, Shannon Craigo-Snell (Craigo-Snell 2015), writing for the Christian Century magazine.

In the article she argued that Jesus is "A Savior, Not a Hero" as if the word hero were an insult. Although the rest of her article is soundly written, denouncing the word hero seems the intent, the effect of which is a constricted definition of hero as a mere rescuer as though that definition of hero fits for everyone. A closer look at Jesus shows him to be a "sometimes rescuer," "sometimes deliverer" and "always a companion through the worst of things" depending on the need. A simple definition of heroism like that of Andy Rooney, might well be a definition Jesus would own up to for himself.

Extreme Heroism reminds us of extreme sports. Like extreme heroism, extreme sports means risking physical life, but not necessarily for someone else. Extreme heroism isn't always that big a risk to physical life although it clearly can be. More often it means risk to our emotional well-being, our mental health and/or spiritual life. Extreme heroism isn't outlandish heroism…it simply means *more advanced* behavior in a given situation; it means *perfected behavior* for a moment in time, *well-trained behavior…even faultless, flawless, ideal, or wholistic behavior.* (Webster's College Dictionary 2003).

Extreme heroism is not the same as comic-book heroism where individuals have super-powers like flight, strength or x-ray vision. Extreme heroism relies on ordinary powers, the type that all children have, all adults and elders have. Extreme heroism has no illusions about its own power, but it does trust in there being something extra about exercising the strength of an indwelling hero so that can act in concert with a greater power not their own.

The news media, to their credit, is not shy about using the word heroism. Every day there seem to be more reports of heroism. CTV News reported just yesterday another story that offers to shed some light on the conflict people have with the word hero. A 7-year-old boy was with three of his friends on a ski-lift in Uxbridge, Ontario, when one of his friends lost a ski and as the ski fell from the lift he turned abruptly in his seat to see where the ski was going and started to slide out of the lift himself. The hero of the story grabbed hold of this friend who by now was dangling half on and half off, holding on for over two long minutes until a rescue team on the ground could bring a net and successfully catch the falling 7-year old who was immediately airlifted to a hospital.

When interviewed by the press, 7-year-old Kostaki Papakonstantinou (Papatonstantinou 2016) said he didn't "feel" like a hero. Like a lot of people he must have concluded therefore that he couldn't be one. Perhaps herein lies a clue to our quest for understanding.

If extreme heroism feels normal to a child then perhaps it feels normal to adults and elders too whenever they do it. Being called heroic may imply to everyone that they are being recognized for having done something abnormal, so they resist…knowing they haven't done anything that felt abnormal. This may explain why phrases like "do the right thing" have come to serve as language bridges because when we say this everyone immediately seems to know or think they know what we mean, therefore no further explanation is necessary "it felt normal" and it was "the right thing to do". Without the language of religion or the language of spirituality, we must turn to simpler language to express our feelings about our deepest and most profound experiences.

In order that this book be usable as a teaching tool, there is at the conclusion of each story/illustration an analysis which identifies (1) injustice motivating the hero to act and (2) evidence that responses were guided by indiscourageable good will for all involved. For example: **(1) The image of a friend dying or being severely injured is an image of an impending injustice. "Here we are having fun, playing in the snow with skis. It would just be plain wrong to let that happen so long as I have the strength to fend against it" might be a child's thought about such an image. (2) Kostaki's response suggests the strength of his good will toward his friend and even his other friends aboard the ski lift.**

Extreme Heroism's Place in the Larger Picture of Heroism

Since we know instinctively there are many forms of heroism we naturally want to know where extreme heroism fits into heroism's big picture. Those familiar with the use of a continuum will know that a continuum is a graphic way of depicting a vast range of related things, like all the ways that our actions qualify as heroism. A continuum of heroism would show, for example, all the ways there for risking one life for the sake of another life, which is limitless but it does provide us with a picture of what we're trying to describe and how this particular subject fits in.

Extreme heroism, out of all the forms of heroism there are, is especially noble. It describes something which everyone would be proud to have as an epitaph on their tombstone. Extreme heroism always has two parts to it: (1) the first is our response to injustice and (2) the second is the principle of good will which shapes and guides our response.

The injustice may occur in the nursery or the bedroom, the playground or the classroom, the boardroom or the marketplace, the living room, the sanctuary or the mosque. The response to this injustice must be born of good will for all and sustained by that same good will. It can flourish anywhere; it has been honored by every race, religion and nation.

The chapters which follow will define in considerable detail this narrow yet super-significant part of life. Look for many true stories of extreme heroism that span age, gender, physical condition, racial, religious and economic boundaries. Some will seem too simple, but that's the way much extreme heroism happens. The real challenge is in letting extreme heroism define one's lifestyle.

WORKS CITED

Webster's College Dictionary. Barnes & Noble Books, 2003.

Craigo-Snell, Shannon. "A Savior, Not a Hero." *Christian Century*, July 15, 2015.

Graves, Ginny. "Is There an Upside to Tragedy?: Yes, say psychologists. It's called post-traumatic growth." *Oprah Magazine, The*, July 2015: 74-75.

Holy Bible, The New Revised Standard Version. New York: Cambridge University Press, 1997.

Papatonstantinou, Kostaki, interview by Kendra Christian and Marigione Commiso (February 12, 2016).

Rooney, Andy. Annual Memorial Day Reflection, New York: CBS 60 Minutes, 2009.

Shaben, Carol. *Into The Abyss: How a Deadly Plane Crash Changed the Lives of a Pilot, a politician, a Criminal and a Cop.* Toronto: Random House Canada, 2012.

Williamson, Marianne. *A Return To Love: Reflections on the Principles of "A Course in Miracles".* New York, NY: HarperCollins, 1992.

CHAPTER 1

CONSPICUOUS BY ABSENCE; UNIFYING BY PRESENCE

How the Word Hero Finally Got My Attention

Like many English-speaking people I grew up with the word hero a natural part of my vocabulary. It was a word I respected. Heroism in my mind was linked to friends of my parents and other adults who had gone off to fight in World War II, who then returned home, wearing their uniforms. I saw them honored publicly in parades and in private gatherings with friends; sometimes they proudly showed their war souvenirs from Europe and the Pacific Islands.

Audie Murphy, a war veteran turned movie actor in those days, was portrayed on the big screen as Hollywood's version of what and who heroes were. I thought of him whenever I heard the word hero. Besides the movies there were also glimpses of heroes in comic books like Superman, Wonder Woman, Bat Man & Robin portraying people with exceptional gifts and super-powers.

I remember wanting to be a hero like Audie Murphy. Being like Superman was out of the question because I didn't possess superpowers, but heroism like Audie Murphy's appeared accessible through the armed services. By the time I was 30 years old however, I had been in and out of the Army and heroism had not yet happened or so I thought.

Some might argue that I was still looking for a way to be a hero when I entered seminary in 1973 to train for professional ministry, to which I would answer "possibly; subconsciously maybe." In seminary it was common to hear discussions about clergy who had a "messiah complex" which meant someone mistaking himself/herself for Jesus, which was repugnant to me. Of course it was also true that it had never occurred to me to think of Jesus as a hero.

Now I have no difficulty thinking of Jesus that way because I regard extreme heroism as a valid way of describing his life. Perhaps he was an extreme hero whose heroic impulses emerged for him just as they do from time to time with all human beings, but in his case it came to dominate his life. It is agreed by many that whatever happened and however we describe it his way of life changed the world for the better.

When I finished seminary and started serving churches in 1976 it was another twenty-five years before I gave further thought to the concept of heroism. It was during those twenty-five years that I grew more conversant with the Greek language. Studies of the Greek language Bible each week, 40 to 50 weeks every year for 30 years had become an important base for interpreting scripture and functioning professionally: writing/preaching sermons, designing/leading public services and responding to human need through pastoral counseling. I would never claim to be a Greek scholar but I did acquire considerable familiarity, professional competency and great enthusiasm for using Biblical Greek for interpretation.

It was during one of those weekly exercises in 2005, which I continue to do in retirement, that I first noticed how the English word hero had become conspicuous by its absence from English language versions of the Bible (Holy Bible, The New Revised Standard Version 1997). Yes. Absence of the word hero and all its forms…is what finally got my attention.

Thinking that my translation might be defective, I turned to other English interpretations of the Bible only to find the same omission in all of them. I took down a reference book from the shelf known as the exhaustive concordance, an extra-large volume containing all the

English words of the Bible (Strong's Exhaustive Concordance 1984), but the English word hero was not listed there either. (The excerpt below depicts a portion of a page from the exhaustive concordance with a red asterisk showing where one would expect the English word hero to be listed but it isn't:

HERMES
HERMOGENES
HERMON
HERMONITES *
HEROD
HERODIANS
HERODIAS
HERODIAS (Strong's Exhaustive Concordance 1984)
**Here is the point where the English word 'hero' should occur in a Concordance were it part of our English Christian vocabulary.*

Many questions emerged: (1) "Given the English word hero is missing from English language Bibles, why isn't the Greek word 'ιεροσ* also missing from the original Greek manuscripts?" (2) "Even though the Greek word 'ιεροσ is used in the Greek language Bible, why is it used so sparingly, given that Greek heroism was so fully developed and deeply embedded in that ancient culture?" (3) "What was wrong, if anything, with the Greek word 'ιεροσ?' and furthermore what was wrong with the English word hero?" When pronounced correctly 'ιεροσ even sounds like the English word 'heroes'.

I remember sitting very still in my office as that day of recognition wore on…unable to function…not knowing what to do next or what to make of the omission. It seemed like it might be important, but was it really? The mystery deepened as I turned to my Webster's Collegiate Dictionary and found the English word hero listed on the same line, alongside its Greek counterpart, 'ιεροσ. (Webster's College Dictionary 2003). If Webster recognized this equivalency, why not The New Revised Standard Translation or the other translations?

That page from Webster looked something like the following: ["He-ro\ 'he-ro, 'hier-o\ n. pl heroes…[Latin heros, from Greek heros]". (Webster's College Dictionary 2003). I pressed on with concern that some great injustice had been done…that maybe English-speaking cultures had been deprived. With new found energy I began finding answers to my questions in a mammoth-sized work by a German lexicographer of biblical languages, Gerhard Kittel, who produced nine related volumes before his death in 1948, cataloging extensive definitions of each Greek word in the Bible. He had nothing to say about English language Bibles, but here's what he said about 'ιεροσ in the Greek language Bible: (Kittel 1968) "The reason that 'ιεροσ occurs so seldom in the NT is a sign that primitive Christianity, from the 1st to the 5th century, shared the linguistic sense of the LXX.*"

> * [Septuagint—a translation of the Hebrew Bible into Koine Greek, made for Egyptian Jews in the 3rd and 2nd centuries BCE and later adopted by the early Christians. Koine Greek was a type of so-called common Greek used in the first century, BCE.]

Kittel explained the limited used of the Greek 'ιεροσ as "rooted in their fear of the sacral words of paganism." By using "primitive" and "afraid of paganism" he suggests the ancients were phobic about the word 'ιεροσ. He describes their fear "anchored in a Greek mythology of deity and nature; a painful reminder of all that a Christian must reject as idolatrous." This in Kittel's opinion was the ancient rationale for restricted usage of 'ιεροσ.

(The following insert depicts a portion of the Greek Analytical Lexicon (Analytical Greek Lexicon, The 1972) and one of the effects of their zeal to restrict usage of the Greek word 'ιεροσ. In italics are several Greek derivatives of 'ιεροσ. The italicized words are mine in order to illustrate some of the consequences of these ancient restrictions when Greek was translated into English in the 13th century.)

Greek Language	Thirteen Centuries later this would be replaced by:
‘ιεροσ–	hallowed; holy, divine…*but not heroic*
‘ιερατεια, ‘ιερατευω -	priesthood…*but not hero-hood*
‘ιερευσ -	priest…*but not hero*
‘ιερον –	temple...*but not place of heroes*
‘Ιεροσολυμα	Jerusalem…*but not city of holy heroes*

Keep in mind that the words “hallowed, holy, divine, priesthood, priest, temple, sacred, and even the city name, Jerusalem, were lofty words in Greek, yet as lofty as they were, scholars of the 13 century were still afraid of the English word hero and so it never appeared in print. Yet when ‘ιεροσ does appears in Greek language Bibles we find examples like the following: “So also Christ did not glorify himself in becoming a high [‘ιεροσ] priest, but was appointed by the one who said to him, “You are my Son, today I have begotten you; as he says also in another place, “You are a [‘ιεροσ] priest forever, according to the order of Melchizedek.” Hebrews, 5:5-6 (Holy Bible, The New Revised Standard Version 1997)

> * Melchizedek is the name given in Hebrew and Christian scripture for a reoccurring personality that precedes Jesus, possibly the same hero figure emerging repeatedly in others throughout human history. In Jesus however, the hero Melchizedek was thought by Christians to reside more fully in him than in any other human being.

Note the novel thing that happens to the meaning of the same verses when the English ‘hero’ is substituted for the Greek: “So also Christ did not glorify himself in becoming a high hero, but was appointed by the one who said to him, ‘you are my Son, today I have begotten you; as he says also in another place, You are a hero forever, according to the order of Melchizedek.’” English-speaking Christians have grown up in every generation without the word hero in their bibles and for the most part, their conversation.

If Kittel was correct in his assumptions about the fate of ‘ιεροσ, that heroism for the most part was considered pagan and evil, then subsequent generations of Christians had no choice but grow up with the understanding that saint, priest, holy, disciple and apostle were the only words that validly named the extraordinary goodness in humanity leaving the word heroism at very least, suspect. Paul Archambault (see Prologue) and countless others through no fault of their own may have been unwitting victims of these ancient decisions to limit and exclude the English word hero. The dialogue Paul needed to hear, was dialogue between those comfortable with hero language and those comfortable with religious language or spiritual language, a conversation that countless others have yet to hear.

The unquestionable reality of that cold winter night in Alberta in 1984 and the aftermath of a plane crash, was that a burst of heroism worthy of any language or religion rose up from within a man named Paul Archambault, disconnecting him from all his apparent faults, enabling him to take responsibility for three strangers and do the right thing. Faced with an extreme hero's choice to take responsibility for others, or not, Paul chose to walk in the way of the great ones of history…at least for a little while.

Beginning the Conversation: Extreme Heroes, Saints, Spirit-Filled

Extreme heroes and others just like them by other names in other cultures are “made of the same right stuff” and “cut from the same cloth”. Would that they could talk to each other and share the wisdom they have acquired. They would realize that everyone spends much of their time doing small good things that later add up to great good things and its all heroic.

But their good deeds are overlooked, taken for granted, even by their nearest beneficiaries. Both learn eventually that through constancy of effort in the passage of time these early effects of extreme heroism have a way of accumulating potency and power. They are the ones who can actually change the world for the better.

Elaine Puckett, Adjunct Professor at Candler School of Theology, Atlanta, Georgia, was writing of extreme heroism when she described it perfectly in her United Methodist Church Blog, saying: "When we think about laying down a life for another we usually think in terms of a singular event but it is possible for us to lay down our lives over the course of a lifetime, minute by minute and day by day. And it is the work of the Spirit to empower us as we seek to lose ourselves in acts of lovingkindness and sacrificial living." (Puckett 2010)

Paul Hawken, described as an environmentalist, entrepreneur, journalist, prolific author and participant in the Civil Rights Movement, wrote: "What I see everywhere in the world are ordinary people willing to confront despair, power, and incalculable odds in order to restore some semblance of grace, justice, and beauty to this world." (Hawken, 2007) His description is a perfect description of extreme heroism… people everywhere responding to despair, abuse of power and against great odds taking action in order to make things right again. It is evidence of the indwelling hero and inner light in everyone.

Just before turning to the elemental forms of extreme heroism in Chapter 2 let me state what should be obvious about my own views: that being Christian as I write this does not mean that I regard extreme heroism as the private domain of Christianity or any other religion. It would be beneficial for everyone to know the equivalent synonyms in Islam, Buddhism, Hinduism, Sikhism, and other world religions.

A wondrous thing about extreme heroism, when its larger forms capture public attention, it gives great pleasure to everyone who sees it. It unifies. Everyone enthusiastically responds to extreme heroism when they see it or hear about it because it brings everyone together. People on every side of any heroic event can be seen nodding and saying "Yes… that was heroic and it's good being human!"

And as you might expect, it hasn't been easy to find examples of those who readily embrace being recognized a hero, but here's one that was reported recently of a young man named Chris O'Gorman, a cab-driver in Nelson, B.C. He was honored recently in Vancouver, by the Canadian Lifesaving Society for saving the life of an 84-year-old man whose boat had tipped over in the Kootenay River. According to a reporter (Johnson 2015) for the Nelson Star, O'Gorman responded to hero recognition in an uncharacteristic but highly recommended way: "I feel good to have had the opportunity to be in the right place at the right time and to help someone. For sure I feel good about it, because I was helping a dude in serious trouble." (O'Gorman 2015)

In order that this book be usable as a teaching tool, there is at the conclusion of each story/illustration an analysis which identifies (1) injustice motivating the hero to act and (2) evidence that responses were guided by indiscourageable good will for all involved. **(1) You don't have to be an accomplished swimmer to see the injustice in a man about to drown. The pain of it. The terror of it. (2) Chris's response to a drowning man, both physically and emotionally, reeks of indiscourageable good will as he observes that it was a privilege to respond and that the victim was a "dude"...worth the effort.**

WORKS CITED

Analytical Greek Lexicon, The. Grand Rapids, MI: Zondervan Publishing House, 1972.

Hawken, Paul. *Blessed Unrest: How the Largest Social Movement in History is Restoring Grace, Justice and Beauty to the World.* New York, New York: Penguin Group (USA), 2007.

Holy Bible, The New Revised Standard Version. New York: Cambridge University Press, 1997.

Johnson, Will. "Hero Honored for 'Stroke of Luck'." *Nelson Star, Nelson, B.C., Canada*, March 20, 2015: 1.

Kittel, Gerhard. *Kittel's Theological Dictionary of the New Testament.* Grand Rapids, MI: Wm. B. Eerdmans Publishing Company, 1968.

O'Gorman, Chris, interview by Will Johnson. *Stroke of Luck* (March 20, 2015).

Puckett, Elaine. "Sojourners." February 15, 2010. sojo.net (accessed March 15, 2015).

Strong's Exhaustive Concordance. Nashville, TN: Thomas Nelson Publishers, 1984.

Webster's College Dictionary. New York, NY: Barnes & Noble Publishers, 2003.

> "Justice in the life and conduct of the State is possible only as first it resides in the hearts and souls of the citizens."
> – **Plato** *(427 BC - 347 BC) Greek philosopher*

CHAPTER 2

EXTREME HEROISM AND INJUSTICE/JUSTICE ARE INSEPARABLE

The first thing that sets extreme heroism apart from other forms of heroism is its relationship to injustice and justice. It is partly a response at an emotional level to seeing an injustice, hearing of an injustice or otherwise experiencing an injustice. If there's no injustice involved then whatever follows is not extreme heroism.

It was injustice Debbie H. Deane wrote about when she said, "Our communities bear witness to the wounding effects of racism, prejudice, intolerance, evil, and injustice of all sorts."

By "bearing witness" Debbie meant continual response to an injustice by naming it, exposing it and otherwise calling attention to it. Having done that an extreme hero looks for responses which promise to restore justice. She said, "We are called to see with God's eyes and be awakened to the reality of the world around us. We are also called to be God's presence in this world, to be a part of the answer to its problems. We are not to be silent but are called, in some way, to take a stand." (Deane, 2011)

Debbie echoes words uttered by holocaust survivor Elie Wiesel who wrote, "There may be times when we are powerless to prevent injustice, but there must never be a time when we fail to protest." (Weisel, 2011) Although some forms of extreme heroism can be difficult to do because they involve degrees of risk and danger, it's important to note that not every risky and dangerous act is necessarily an appropriate response to injustice. Climbing Mount Everest, for example, is risky and dangerous…considered heroic by many, but Mount Everest just being there doesn't constitute an injustice. Conquering Mount Everest may indeed be heroic but that doesn't make it extremely heroic, because extreme heroism is inseparable from injustice/justice.

When injustice is the key to identifying extreme heroism then we soon learn that extreme heroism begins as we sense something unfair in the lives of others and/or in our own lives. There usually follows an inner prompting to do something about the injustice. When that happens (initial emotional pain followed by inner prompting) we can say with confidence that we have been summoned to the threshold of extreme heroism where we will be required to make even more decisions.

When PBS presented a four-hour documentary in 2016 on the life of baseball legend Jackie Robinson (Burns, 2016) they told a story not only of a gifted man who excelled in every sport, as a military officer, eventually in business, but also one who could not ignore the pain of racial prejudice toward himself and all African Americans. No amount of success, accolade, fame or even fortune could dull that pain and so all of his life became response after response after response to those injustices, primarily verbal and non-violent. His fans were torn between supporting him for his courage on the baseball field and wishing that he would stop verbalizing off the field.

Robinson's wife, Rachel Isum Robinson, was the ideal partner for an extreme hero…an extreme hero herself in advising, supporting her husband. Long after his death she is still advocating for his ideals.

Extreme hero and 2004 Nobel Peace Prize recipient Wangari Maathai (Maathai, 2011) described his own inner promptings to be unrelenting in response to injustice this way: "I don't really know why I care so much. I just have something inside me that tells me that there is a problem, and I have got to do something about it. I think that is what I would call the God in me." Wangari understood this inner prompting as divine in origin.

If an injustice is to be responded to it must first be recognized; it is our inner sensitivity to injustice that puts us on alert. A young mother writing in her annual Christmas letter to her larger family reflected on a 3-year-old son's emergent behavior during the year: "He really lets us know now when he thinks a family rule has been violated or a family promise has been broken. He holds us accountable and won't let us get away with anything that seems unfair."

Bravo to the mother or the father for recognizing such sensitivity in their children and taking steps to affirm and reinforce it.

In order that this book be usable as a teaching tool, there is at the conclusion of each story/illustration an analysis which identifies (1) injustice motivating the hero to act and (2) evidence that responses were guided by indiscourageable good will for all involved. **(1) These injustices are clearly identified: "a family rule violated"... "a family promise broken". (2) While IGW (indiscourageable good will) is harder to identify with certainty, there has to be a strong level of trust and good will for his family before holding his/her family accountable at the age of 3.**

Obviously not everyone is sensitive to every injustice at the same time and that is a good thing because seeing and feeling all the injustice which crosses our personal paths in a single day would be overwhelming and destructive. Most of us are sensitive in one moment and not in the next because sensitivity comes and goes, but without sensitivity we are likely to not notice. Perhaps some can recognize injustice without experiencing emotional pain, but that would be unusual.

What magnifies the importance of sensitivity to injustice is the fact that it must be applied to both sides of the injustice-justice coin, so to speak; by that I mean there is injustice and its corresponding justice. In other words we need sensitivity to goodness also...sensitivity to fairness, sensitivity to a job well done...even more than sensitivity to what's wrong because both are in play at every turn. A young mother or a young father must be sensitive to those times when their children choose to take a stand for good and willing to affirm those words and deeds which restore justice.

Without sensitivity to justice we won't recognize it when it is achieved. We won't know where we're going or what our goals are. We will never be unable to appreciate the justice that already exists.

The following story illustrates how an injustice first impinges upon most people, even children. It also illustrates sensitivity residing in children. This is a composite of countless similar examples of extreme heroism reported by news media nearly every day:

Having the Sensitivity of a Nine-Year-Old Boy

The skies outside had suddenly turned dark as another line of late-afternoon thunderstorms came marching across so-called tornado alley in Oklahoma. A nine-year-old peered cautiously through the curtained windows of his bedroom as a bolt of lightning sizzled through the air, flashed brightly and exploded with a fierce bang in the front yard where Daddy usually parked his pick-up truck. Daddy was away at work.

The sizzling sound frightened the boy as it would anyone and of course every tabby cat and dog for miles around, sending them all scurrying for cover under the house, barn or into a dark closet somewhere. A few seconds later there was another flash and louder bang that seemed to rock their double-wide trailer-house. The boy moved instinctively in search of comfort and reassurance down the darkened hallway to the kitchen where his mother had been preparing supper. The delightful smell of onions frying hung in the air and told him where he might find her.

Entering the kitchen he was surprised to see there were no lights on but it crossed his mind that maybe the lightning had damaged something. Before he could finish the thought he rounded the corner of the cooking island and saw his mother lying still on the floor. Two things came quickly to his mind: (1) that something was definitely wrong (he wouldn't have called it an injustice, but that's what it was) and (2) that he was the only one available to do something that might make it right again.

Momma couldn't be left lying on the floor like that…it was just wrong. He wanted to see her standing and hear her talking to him, reassuring him. He cautiously touched his mother and said, "Momma?" He paused and gently shook her again, "Momma?"

When she didn't respond the boy's thoughts went into his memory in search of a proper response and came to an evening a few weeks earlier, down the road at the rural church the family attended. Remembering what he was taught that night, how to use a telephone in case of an emergency, he found himself on the threshold of extreme heroism, picking up the telephone, taking a deep breath…and then pressing on to dial 911 just as he had been taught. He would remember everything else that happened that night like it was a dream…talking to a stranger on the phone, giving directions to their home, staying on the line while talking and answering questions about his mother…putting a damp washcloth on Momma's forehead…hearing the EMT vehicle drive into the yard with siren wailing and lights flashing…watching uniformed people attend to Momma…seeing Daddy come home… seeing Momma sit up and then lying on a stretcher as it was being loaded into the EMT vehicle.

With justice partly arrived and partly still arriving, as all of these stages of the story unfolded, along came recognition for the boy's actions…from Momma and Daddy…the neighbors…teachers and kids at school…even a reporter from the community newspaper. By the time the thunderstorms had all passed through, bringing clear skies and a warm sun, he would be called a hero and almost everyone would say, "Amen!" All of us have heard stories of heroes like this, but we may not have known it was about an extreme hero, simply because a child did it.

In order that this book be usable as a teaching tool, there is at the conclusion of each story/illustration an analysis which identifies (1) injustice motivating the hero to act and (2) evidence that responses were guided by indiscourageable good will for all involved. **(1) A mother lying unconscious on the kitchen floor is unjust. It scares us so badly that some can immediately hear an inner prompting to respond. (2) A child decides to trust training received from strangers at a nearby church. He then trusts a voice on the phone asking for personal information he wouldn't ordinarily divulge to strangers.**

Sensitivity to Injustice

An inner aptitude for extreme heroism, which this Oklahoma child probably didn't know was in him, was awakened by the drama and trauma of the moment. It helped a lot that he had the received training which became a channel for his heroic impulses; but above all it was his sensitivity to the situation which signaled to him the words "not right" and "do something to make it right again" with an inner voice that only he could hear. In this case, his was a simple heroic response to turn to a stranger – call someone to come and "Help Momma stand up again ".

He had practiced beforehand like war heroes do in basic training, before responding to actual battlefield injustice....and the training didn't make the boy less of a hero any more than an adult soldier's training makes him/her less a hero in the midst of combat. In fact a lot of injustice in an infinite number of situations can be and should be anticipated. Training should be planned for and implemented with a view toward some predictable injustice occurring in the future.

It appears that human beings are universally 'hard-wired' for detecting injustice; it comes with birth. Unfortunately, the same sensitivity which is so essential, can be dampened...even extinguished, by the experiences of life until some become unresponsive. If not dampened, our sensitivities can be magnified by the experiences of life to such an extent that we lose sight of the many good things (justice) in life; we may become like those who perpetually see the glass half-empty instead of half-full.

Ideally, people want sensitivity and they want it balanced; and by balanced it means 'favoring justice'. Balanced sensitivity comes through socialization and education. Those who are closest to us as we grow up, help develop those sensitivities.

Sensitivity to gender injustice, racial injustice, economic injustice, etc. depend on who influenced us most in childhood – family, teachers, coaches, etc. Continued evolution toward greater and still balanced sensitivity depends on who is nearest as we experience marriage, work, higher education and community service. Other influences include government, military, church, universities, corporations, etc.

All of us at this very moment have arrived at some level of sensitivity to injustice which means most of us are walking, talking antennae arrays of sensitivity; living radars capable of detecting injustice wherever we are. But some grow weary of sensing injustice and tired of thinking about all that seems wrong. They find ways to tune out and turn off through distraction and dulling influences like drugs, alcohol, work, busyness, money, accumulating possessions, etc.

As Diana Rodriguez put it, "We are called to seek justice, not to burn out seeking it. I am not going to fix the world by myself. I have to realize the fact that sometimes I try to do too much and end up doing nothing. My soul will be restored every time my efforts toward environmental, social, or economic justice are put into action, one step at a time." (Rodriguez, 2013)

The Dangerous Dumbing & Dulling Effect of Wealth

"The global economy may be in turmoil but the super-rich aren't suffering." wrote Mark Adams in 2010 (Adams, 2010), saying "The world's millionaires are actually seeing their fortunes rise. The worst effects of the global recession have done little to dent the lifestyles or fortunes of the super-rich." Though written six years ago those who know, tell us this is still true.

Wealth has a reputation for numbing and dumbing down our sensitivities. The conviction that this is dangerous and likely to render us blind is all but lost on the rich but powerfully captured by certain religious teachings: "It will be easier for a camel to pass through the eye of a needle than for a rich man to enter the kingdom of heaven. (Luke 18: 23-25) (Holy Bible, The New Revised Standard Version, 1997) Once sedated by wealth we are more than likely to become oblivious to the suffering of those in poverty like those hedge-fund operators who plundered the savings and pensions of innocent, trusting people who simply wanted to do sensible things with what little money they had. It's like soldiers taught to diminish the enemy's human worth by creating racial slurs to apply to them and names to call them.

While wealth can dull our sensitivity, poverty kills...literally. Poverty is considered by most philosophers, theologians and historians as the greatest single injustice known to humankind because it spawns the worst of all other forms of injustice...murder, rape, war, etc. Adams said in 2010 that one family of four in every fifteen was living in poverty in the United States - which should alert us - arouse our sensitivities - to the injustice which poverty currently imposes upon millions even as we speak. It's killing them.

Our sensitivities may be calling us forth at this very moment to respond to this particular threat through extreme heroic measures whenever and however we can muster them. Failure to respond creatively and lovingly to this economic imbalance in the past has brought about the end to several civilizations before and it will do it again if we do not respond with extreme heroism. "While the world's economic output may have shrunk by two per cent during 2009, the collective wealth of the world's millionaires actually soared by 18.9 per cent, a major new study shows... the ranks of the super-rich are also expanding rapidly." (Adams, 2010).

Just in reading this, our inner radars, if not already desensitized, ought to be setting off loud warning bells. If we know the history of excessive wealth concentrated in the hands of a few in the past - and if we have a pulse - we will find this report alarming.

Fortunately the injustice of poverty has produced many stories of extreme heroism recorded in the sacred literature of many religions... like that of the ancient Hebrews. They tell for example the story of Amos, a poor farmer striving to make ends meet at a time when part of Israel's northern kingdom was enjoying extreme prosperity while another part remained in grinding poverty. His response was one classic example of extreme heroism and a response to injustice.

Being sensitive to what this imbalance would bring upon the nation, Amos, after brooding about it, responded with words...vivid words... words describing a disastrous future for the whole nation (rich and poor) if the injustice wasn't responded to. We should note that it wasn't a violent response. It was more like one of today's responses... "If you see something, say something."

It was meant to rescue a nation, it proved effective and it was via words…potent words…powerful words…words painful for some to hear…words that would hasten the very results he was describing if something didn't change. [The Book of Amos (Holy Bible, The New Revised Standard Version, 1997)]

Many have felt similar pain in recent times when headlines and news videos were reporting 'Occupy Wall Street', 'Occupy Toronto' and in my town…'Occupy Nelson'…people gathering in the most public of places (even in the dead of winter) to discuss and witness to the danger. Word went out during that time all over the continent…word meant to warn us of a dark future if this current economic injustice is allowed to go unchecked.

If our internal radar is unaffected by this story, then keep in mind what some of the great minds in the world have said about the injustice of poverty…that it is a source of unimaginable trauma for millions, producing an overwhelming number of *arrested heroes* (heroes unable to rise to the occasion of injustice set before them - see Section 3, Chapter 15, *Trauma*). The greater the number of arrested heroes, the faster the injustice spreads like a disease. The Greek philosopher Plato said, 'An imbalance between rich and poor is the oldest and most fatal ailment of all republics.' (Plato).

Modern theologian and Peruvian, Gustavo Gutierrez, said "We often see poverty as an economic and social issue, but we must have a deeper understanding. In the ultimate analysis, poverty is death. It is an unjust and early death. It is the destruction of persons, of people, and nations." (Gutierrez, 2000) And that leads us to this sobering thought: that if any of us are the offspring of any of those who endured The Great Depression of the early 1900's in North America then we were raised by victims of that great injustice and may have inherited some of the trauma that came with it.

Thankfully, throughout history, there have been a handful in every time whose great wealth did not blind them completely; who recognized the hazards and great damage being done by wealth in the hands of a few…people like Francesco Pietro Bernardone (1181-1226) who would become St. Francis of Assisi, born to wealth, seeing the danger in time; rejecting the wealth and embracing other values. In our recent past there have been people like the American Roosevelts, President Franklin and First Lady Eleanor (1933-1945) who were wealthy but somehow sensitive to the poor and in our modern time, contemporaries like Bill Gates and Warren Buffet who have acted as extreme heroes responding to injustice with their wealth, risking their lives and livelihood by redirecting their wealth toward the saving of others…and also the newest Pope of The Roman Catholic Church…Argentine Jorge Mario Bergolio, Pope Francis.

Six weeks after beginning a campaign to get other billionaires to donate most of their fortunes, Buffett released the first list of 40 others who have signed what he and Gates call the Giving Pledge. (Blankinship, 2010) Somehow other sensitivities were awakened to the suffering of the poor and some of those in power have been moved to those constructive acts which could restore justice.

WORKS CITED

Adams, M. (2010, July 2). *Where Millionaires Live.* UK: MSN.

Burns, K. (Director). (2016). Jackie Robinson (Motion Picture)

Blankinship, D. G. (2010, August 5). Gates, Buiffett tap billionaires for charity. *The Washington Poast.* Washington, D.C., U.S.: The Washington Post.

Deane, D. H. (2011). *Verse and Voice.* Retrieved 2011, from Sojourners: www.sojo.net

Gutierrez, G. (2000). Dominican Priest, Peruvian Theologian. U.S.: Brown University.

Holy Bible, The New Revised Standard Version. (1997). New York: Cambridge University Press.

Maathai, W. (2011). *Sojourners.* Retrieved 2011, from Verse and Voice: www.sojo.net

Plato. (n.d.). *Verse and Voice.* Retrieved 2010, from Sojourners: www.sojo.net

Rodriguez, D. (2013, October 9). *Sojourners.* Retrieved from Verse and Voice: www.sojo.net

Weisel, E. (2011). *Sojourners.* Retrieved 2011, from Verse and Voice: www.sojo.net

CHAPTER 3

EXTREME HEROISM: IT'S MAGNITUDE

Extreme Heroism Is Most Often Writ Small

Common wisdom understands heroism to be something big, gigantic and enormous; something that blows us away, every time. It can be those things, that's true, but most often acts of extreme heroism are small, tiny, imperceptible and even invisible...yet very real and very potent each time they occur. Do not be offended by the simplicity and size of extreme heroism. It's the essential elements that make it extreme and effective.

Common wisdom also understands heroism as a risk to physical life only. No. Other forms of life are more often at risk: emotional, mental and spiritual life. Fear, sorrow, anger, rage and joy are emotional factors by which risk is measured. Peace, calm, serenity, respect, reverence are some of the mental factors. Patience, kindness, compassion and faith are among the spiritual. All these things are in play at every moment whether the scene is domestic, collegial, neighborhood, church or play.

The 2004-2012 ABC television series *Desperate Housewives* (Cherry, 2004-2012) depicted life in a suburban cul-de-sac where a dozen or so families lived in close proximity. Whether a cul-de-sac like *Wisteria Lane*, an apartment house, a condominium, a neighborhood or a small rural community, one can always count on there being multiple injustices occurring simultaneously...injustices which affect the lives of everyone in the cul-de-sac whether everyone is aware of it or not. It can be injustices to an aging, widowed unmarried couple living together secretly to cut down on housing expenses or all the injustices affecting an upwardly mobile young Latino couple with small children in an all-white neighborhood. It can be an African-American couple with teenagers or a gay couple thinking of adopting or a single-parent trying to make a life for herself and an adult child who has just returned to refill the empty nest.

Everyone face injustices – those inflicted directly and those observed as afflicting others. All injustices deserve extreme heroic responses. Most responses will be conducted face to face between two people and go unnoticed by all the rest. Most responses will be recognized only by the beneficiaries of those responses.

The fact of life about casual communities is that they have lot in common with institutionalized communities or religious orders. Benedictine Nun, Joan Chittister, living in community with other women, committed to daily applications of extreme heroism by another name, wrote, "Every spiritual master in every tradition talks about the significance of small things in a complex world. Small actions in social life, small efforts in the spiritual life, small moments in personal life... all of them become great in the long run, the mystics say, but all of them look like little or nothing in themselves." (Chittister, 2009)

In the examples of extreme heroism which you are about to read therefore do not expect to be overwhelmed. Expect to be underwhelmed in some cases but pay close attention to the potency of things which seem small to insignificant. It's the small things that make everything else sweeter and better. In the process, injustice is replaced with justice and division is replaced by healthy unity.

Extreme Heroes Show Up With Whatever They Have

Lawrence was sitting alone in his home office, working feverishly at his computer to meet a publisher's deadline, when suddenly there was a knock at the door. He reluctantly gets up, walks to the door to open it and sees a young woman standing there whom he recognizes as a newcomer to the neighborhood. Until now he had ignored her but did remember the moving van that had blocked the street for a day while workers unloaded her furniture and family belongings.

As soon as he opened the door it was clear that the woman was delighted, even if he wasn't. She clapped her hands together as if a fervent prayer had been answered and said, "At last! Someone!" And then she went right to it: "Do you have jumper cables?"

Realizing she had started the conversation too abruptly she stopped to apologize and introduce herself as Jenny across the street. She turned to point to where her car was sitting in the driveway, filled with children, sitting in the hot July sun. The battery was dead she explained and said that she had tried several other neighbors before arriving at Lawrence's home.

As a matter of fact Lawrence did have jumper cables, in his car, but it gave him no joy to admit it because he could see where this was going. She was going to ask him to leave his work, go out into the heat himself, get his car out of the garage, move his car across the street, get as close as possible to her car, get out his jumper cables and because he was a man, hook the cables up correctly in order to give her battery the boost needed to start her car. Even as Lawrence started toward his garage he was grumbling to himself, "Why do I have to be the only one home today?"

He continued…"Why am I being called upon to do something I know next to nothing about? Why do I even have jumper cables?!! I might destroy her car AND mine if I hook things up the wrong way! I may look like a man's man, but this will expose me as a fraud. God, do I *HAVE* to do this?"

The answer seemed to be *YES.*

Guided by good will? Well that might seem like a stretch, given all the grumbling he was doing. But yes, sometimes it's good will for others that turns out to be stronger than our ill will and the desire to be left alone. That's often when we tell ourselves later… "I'm glad this happened!"

We do things we do not want to because down deep we want things to go well even for those who impose upon our lives, so like a beaten dog, Lawrence moved robotically toward getting the job done. He backed out of his driveway, moved across the street with his car, drove up on the driveway beside her car, stuck his head under the two hoods, searching first for a place to connect the red cables and then the black cables.

He went through the motions, straightened up, stepped back, cringed and called out to her sitting in her car: "OK! Give it try!" Her car started the very first turn of the ignition! Lawrence disconnected and rolled up his jumper cables, shaking his head in amazement, astounded that it had worked and…grateful.

The woman closed the hood to her SUV and turned to him saying fervently: "You're my hero! You *ARE* my hero!" Lawrence blushed! He struggled with the weight of that title because he considered it a kind of a miracle that anything good had happened at all. All he had done was show up, bring what he had, go through the motions…the extra something else that showed up seemed to materialize as it was needed… some people call that luck…some call it providence…some don't call it anything, but they notice it.

Often that's way extreme heroism happens…we show up, bring what we have, go through the motions, something more happens and sometimes we're surprised…blown away. The woman lingered, smiled at Lawrence…then got into her SUV, backed out of the driveway onto the asphalt shimmering with heat, perhaps sensing she had done him a favor by asking for his help. The children waved to Lawrence from the back window as their mother drove them away in air-conditioned comfort. Justice appeared to be restored once again.

Much that qualifies as extreme heroism seems hidden, happening between two people, going unnoticed yet coloring our feelings about our various communities. Fortunately for Lawrence, his actions were noticed by Jenny and she gave them a proper name…heroism. Technically it all began with Jenny's courageous response to an injustice imposed on her who then responded by asking a stranger for help.

Lawrence felt good as he returned his car to his own driveway and returned to his writing not knowing he had walked the way of extreme heroes, even if only for a few minutes. "In matters of truth and justice," said Albert Einstein, "there is no difference between large and small problems, for issues concerning the treatment of people are all the same." (Einstein, 2013)

In order that this book be usable as a teaching tool, there is at the conclusion of each story/illustration an analysis which identifies (1) injustice motivating the hero to act and (2) evidence that responses were guided by indiscourageable good will for all involved. For example: **(1) The injustice of a car whose battery has gone dead without warning is obvious and compounded by the presence of small children in a hot car. (2) the mother must have had good will for her own sake as well as that of her children. (3) The injustice of interrupting a professional writer with deadlines to meet is obvious. (4) His good will toward a new neighbor is certainly limited but it is enough to overcome his understandable ill will. His ill will is close to winning but a residual obligation to do the right thing overrides his urge to ignore her needs.**

Extreme Heroism in the Snow on a Safeway Parking Lot

It was a cold, crisp winter evening; the kind where the snow crunches noisily beneath your feet as you walk and the cold air calls forth a frosty cloud from your nose each time you breathe. It was getting dark and the parking lot was full with the usual on-the-way-home-from-work grocery shoppers along with 54-year-old Marge Sterling who had just finished a quick shop for supper. It was dark as she finished with the cashier and pushed her cart through the automatic doors out onto a snow-packed parking lot.

Having relocated her car, over to the far side of the lot, Marge began moving toward it, pushing the cart where snow had been cleared and at the same time searching through her purse for car keys. There was no hint of the danger approaching her from behind…only the sudden sound of an automobile engine where it shouldn't be – immediately to her right and down at her hip! Instinctively Marge looked to the right and side-stepped to the left as the passing car brushed her clothing and continued on without pausing.

Inside the car was 92-year-old Edith James, leaning forward, peering out through thick glasses looking for a place to park; Marge in the meantime stood riveted to the spot trying to fathom what had just happened and almost happened. Her eyes fastened on Edith's car as it had moved around the lot finally coming to a stop. If Marge seemed paralyzed, it was not because she was hurt physically, but because somehow she felt violated...something wrong/unjust had just happened. It didn't leave a mark on her, but she was still a victim. The life she would soon risk in responding would not be physical, but emotional and spiritual.

Two other shoppers, both male, happened to be on the parking lot when all this happened and they too had held their breath as the car rolled by. Now they were holding their breath awaiting a response from this woman who neither of them knew. Would she move to her car, unload groceries and drive away?

Would she respond passively and absorb the pain of this injustice? Or would she do something creative? Both men were beside themselves having seen this injustice with their own eyes. Both wanted justice restored, even if she didn't.

Without knowing Marge's history, the two men could not predict what she would do but chances were high that she would do what many others do in similar situations – nothing. Like many before her she would probably repress her feelings, decide that the thing which had happened was 'no problem'...'no harm, no foul'. But if she continued with that scenario it might occur to her later that not-doing anything could impose a worse injustice on someone else.

It occurred to Marge that she might go to where the woman parked in order to 'raise her voice' at her as she got out of her car. Many are those who have tried responding to injustice this way ...trumping one injustice with another injustice. But if Marge had been the beneficiary of hero education and training – she might do something heroic. She might call the police...get the law involved...or respond like a prophet with words designed to convey the truth even if it hurts to hear it. She might decide that this woman will suffer enough just by speaking to her with the respect due someone her age, drawing words out of gentle storage, wanting the best for this woman, herself and unseen others.

Here is what actually happened: The two men who had been on the parking lot watching as the injustice unfolded felt compelled to do more than just walk away. They moved toward Marge to see if she was injured* and to make sure she was otherwise OK. When she affirmed that she was alright, one of the men turned toward his car satisfied that nothing more was needed.

> (*These two also responded with extreme heroism...tiny perhaps, but imperceptibly potent for Marge.)

The other man lingered...because Marge had not yet moved. Time seemed to stand still as together they talked about what had happened... verbalizing and reliving the injustice. When the question finally came up about what she should do, Marge said "Someone ought to talk to her." The man asked her if she wanted his company while she did that. She hesitated and then said "No. I can do it myself."

With that she left her grocery cart by her car and walked to Edith's parking spot. Their conversation was inaudible across the snow-covered parking lot but the clouds of their breath could be seen in the light from a lamp post. They talked for two...maybe three minutes. Then Edith reached out to touch Marge with what looked like a gesture of gratitude.

Edith went on into the grocery store; Marge went back to her car and the cart still full of groceries. It's hard to say for sure sometimes, but this time it appeared that an injustice had been addressed, corrected, wrong had been changed to a right and a future injustice had been averted. All four people involved responded with extreme heroism. Perhaps all who remember this incident will realize they each had a part in making a particular wrong, right; and for all their efforts they had made the community a better place in which to live.

In order that this book be usable as a teaching tool, there is at the conclusion of each story/illustration an analysis which identifies (1) injustice motivating the hero to act and (2) evidence that responses were guided by indiscourageable good will for all involved. For example: **(1) A shopper almost hit by a passing car is not the same injustice as a shopper actually hit, but it is still an injustice. A prior injustice seems evident in someone licensed to drive a car long after they should be. These injustices ignored or overlooked can lead to a greater injustice at some other time. (2) The victim seems to be thumbing through all the possible responses she knows and finally settles on one that seems guided by indiscourageable good will.**

Extreme Heroism and the Unjust Plumber

Bob and Sue were professional musicians who made a living playing gigs at local motel lounges, taverns and clubs. They weren't rich by any means but they were living comfortably. They were pretty self-aware people who knew their own strengths, weaknesses and limitations. They knew for example that they couldn't fix things in their house or car if anything happened to break, so they often 'farmed' those kinds of things out to people who were skilled and gifted at fixing.

They didn't mind doing this…paying others to do something better than they could…only seemed fair. They considered this to be the way the world worked and functioned best. They suffered no delusions that they should be able to do everything for themselves.

So when the upstairs bathroom faucet and the downstairs kitchen faucet started leaking simultaneously and profusely the same morning, they called a friend who had his own plumbing business. "I can't come for a few days" he said and apologized for being so busy; there had been a flurry of plumbing needs around town and so he referred them to another friend. So they called the friend's friend and left a message on the answering machine which mentioned that this was a referral, outlining their needs, left a phone number, address and their names.

Two days later, when there had been no answer, Bob and Sue called again and getting the answering machine again they left a 2nd message.

Meanwhile the plumbing leaks were getting worse. After a while they called a third time and left a third message*.

> (*Take a moment to be aware of the mounting injustices here and each stage of compounding; also be aware of the victim's response.)

When again there was no response Bob and Sue got out the telephone directory and paged through until they found an address for their friend's friend and drove to that address. The address was residential but signage indicated a plumbing service being operated from someone's home. There was a van in the garage and a car parked in front of the house, so they parked in the driveway behind the van and walked up to a side door designated 'office' and rang the doorbell.

An unsmiling middle-aged woman with black horn-rimmed glasses wearing coveralls with a company logo emblazoned over the pocket came to the screen-door and peered out. Bob and Sue identified themselves and said they had called several times and there had been no answer. "Because a friend recommended you we wanted to give you every chance to respond."

The woman responded rather flatly, "Yes, I remember your calls." "We've been so busy with major calls from around the area we just haven't had anyone free to respond, but I will send one our emergency plumbers over this afternoon. Sorry for the inconvenience."

Bob and Sue returned home wondering if this would turn out the same way their other efforts did but a few minutes later the phone rang. It was the emergency plumber wanting to make an appointment for later that afternoon. He came and in a few minutes had both faucets repaired.

As the emergency plumber drove away he said his contractor would be sending a bill. When no bill was forthcoming two weeks later, Bob called the first plumber to say they had not received a bill. The woman on the other end of the line said "There won't be any charges."

"Now why is that?" Bob asked. "That doesn't seem fair."

"The woman said, "It's just something we want to do." And then she added, "If there are any other problems give us a call." In keeping with her other social skills she abruptly hung up.

Often extreme heroism requires enormous patience. Not everyone in business for themselves has all the social skills that are needed. They have no sense of the hurt and harm they inflict by their silence and much of the time with them it seems as though nothing good is happening. It's as if we're walking down a path with many tests, twists, turns, forks and then, after what seems like an exceedingly long time, you arrive... somewhere...and somewhere is better than the place where you began.

Perhaps that's what every injustice/justice feels like within a family, within a workplace, within a community as its being restored...small things, small hurts, small moments of suffering, small inconveniences swelling and threatening to explode but someone turns it around, does an extremely heroic thing and suddenly the community is better again. It's that way at every level of human existence, between friends, between family members all the way to nations working to solve monumental issues concerning national security, economy, law and order.

In order that this book be usable as a teaching tool, there is at the conclusion of each story/illustration an analysis which identifies (1) injustice motivating the hero to act and (2) evidence that responses were guided by indiscourageable good will for all involved. For example: **(1) A professional not behaving professionally is an injustice. Repeated professional neglect is even more unjust. (2) Victims of unprofessional behavior are often required to summon enormous patience. It can be like water dripping on stone, but eventually, with real dripping water, the water wins.**

Extreme Heroism and the Unjust Doggies

Phyllis and Brad, after 30 years of renting, finally saved enough for a down-payment on their first house. It was a charming two-story house with a basement, an unattached two-car garage in 'old-town' just a short walk from the center of downtown. The yard had space for lawn in front, lawn in back and a garden.

They took great pleasure in driving down the back lane, pressing the garage door opener as they approached, watching the door open as if to welcome them home. As they soon learned however, not everything was as welcoming as that garage door because living next door to them were four self-appointed watch-dogs who gathered on the opposite side of the chain-link fence to watch their every movement whether departing or arriving. As soon as Phyllis or Brad opened the side door to the garage the dogs would begin barking loudly, urgently, continuously, with all the excitement that four barking dogs can muster…until Phyllis and Brad had walked from the detached garage and reached the back door of their house.

It took some of the pleasure out of home ownership and coming home. At first they thought, the dogs would eventually get used to them and allow them a free pass instead of barking like they were thieves. Not so. A year later the ferocious four still gathered together at the fence waiting for the side door to the garage to open and then announcing to the whole neighborhood that outsiders had returned to the house next to theirs…again.

As Brad pondered heroic ways to respond to this injustice, he thought of talking to the neighbor, but was reluctant to do that because he didn't know what to suggest his neighbor do. It never occurred to him that he might have suggestions of his own, but one day while shopping at the local hardware store displaying camping gear and other summer items, his gaze landed on a so-called 'super-soaker'…a water squirt gun shaped like a rifle with a large capacity, yellow, holding tank. He smiled to himself as he stood at the check-out counter thinking about what he would do the next time he arrived home.

As it happened, just as he was arriving home, as 'fate' or 'providence' would have it, the neighbor next door, owner of the dogs, happened to be outside clearing weeds along his part of the back lane. Brad slowed the car as he approached, lowered the window and stopped so they could talk. He showed his neighbor the super-soaker sitting on the seat beside him and told the neighbor what he was planning…would the neighbor be OK with that? The neighbor said "Of course!"

Continuing on to his garage Brad turned in and parked. The dogs greeted him as per usual as he walked to the house. Brad smiled in contemplation as he opened the kitchen door and went inside to fill the soaker with water.

He walked outside. The dogs rushed to the fence barking. Brad strode straight for them, aiming and squirting…soaking the dogs on the first pump.

They yelped as if in pain, turned and ran to their kennels to hide. It worked! The dogs learned to recognize the super-soaker as soon as it appeared and either went silent or into hiding.

After a while only one of the four dogs persisted in barking every time they came home but as soon as Brad started storing the soaker in the garage, so that the dogs saw the soaker as soon as the side door opened, that dog learned to be silent too. A few years later, after Brad and Phyllis sold the house and moved to another town for new jobs they continued to wonder what became of the dogs after they left and how they treated the new owners.

Years later when Brad and Phyllis happened to be visiting their old neighborhood they turned down the lane that would take them past their old garage. There in their neighbor's yard was another garage… new and where the dog kennels used to be. The dogs now enjoyed new kennels on the opposite side of the neighbor's yard.

A fortuitous moment responded to appropriately, had offered up a solution to a difficult situation that morning when Brad returned from the hardware store, stopping to seek permission from his neighbor to use the super-soaker…not imposing another injustice on injustice. Brad may have opened the door to changes that would benefit future owners and neighbors. It also paved a way for Brad and Phyllis to depart the neighborhood in a relationship of mutual respect with the neighbors. Even the doggies next door had benefitted.

In order that this book be usable as a teaching tool, there is at the conclusion of each story/illustration an analysis which identifies (1) injustice motivating the hero to act and (2) evidence that responses were guided by indiscourageable good will for all involved. For example: **(1) Dogs barking at the next door neighbor is an obvious injustice. (2) Seizing an opportunity to test a harmless solution with the neighbor reveals good will. Although the solution was not a permanent one, it may have paved the way to a more permanent solution for a future neighbor.**

The Second Most Important Thing about Extreme Heroism

The second most important thing we know about extreme heroism – the first being its relationship to injustice - is being aware of its size and its significance, even in its smallest expression. Popular thought holds that all heroism is big, bigger and biggest, when actually extreme heroism knows no size limits in either direction. While more often small, tiny and even invisible at the emotional, thinking or spiritual levels it CAN grow to have immense influence before becoming visible. The following is a story involving two men and the extreme heroism which led to one of them becoming Canada's first Prime Minister.

Big Yet Small

There are times in the life of every nation when extreme heroes emerge while doing something that gets widespread attention because it IS big. Many Canadians and Americans know the name John A. MacDonald as the first Prime Minister of Canada and consider him a national hero, but few will think of him as extreme hero. At the same time almost no one, even in Canada, will the know the name George Brown or that his extreme heroism may have been greater than that of John A MacDonald. At very least, Brown was a co-contributor to extreme heroism in the mid-1860s just prior to Canada becoming Canada.(Gwyn, 2007)

EVERYONE should know the name George Brown who may have been an extreme hero of greater proportions than John A. MacDonald. Here's why: In the 1860s, before Canada became Canada, John A. and George were political protagonists – arch rivals pitted against each other for the leadership of a nation yet unnamed. Their public behavior toward one another while pursuing the honor of leading a new nation, while acceptable to the parliamentarians of the time, bordered on mutual destruction…their words were cutting, cruel, dripping with sarcasm; they traded injustices through their words like two soldiers standing toe to toe while firing their weapons at each other, close range.

MacDonald was a lawyer and a career politician. Brown was a writer and the editor of *The Globe Newspaper* which would later become the famous *Globe and Mail Newspaper* of Toronto, Ontario. Their public language and rhetoric was personal and ugly as they jockeyed for leadership, but it would soon depend on a better use of privacy to solve their conflict. Fortunately for them and the nation, compromise was not a dirty word, not for John A. nor for George.

The injustice to which they were both responding originally was a disorganized conglomeration of North American geographies belonging to England. The justice/greater good they saw waiting for them was a unified nation called Canada. MacDonald and Brown's behavior morphed at just the right time from mutually assured destruction to something brave, courageous, and extremely heroic.

Both Macdonald and Brown had sizeable followings of representatives from various parts of the country. Each could probably count on about 50 percent of the electorate. It was a political tie any way one looked at it.

Macdonald, to his credit, was the first to step away from the destructive path and Brown was courageous enough to join him. MacDonald came to Brown privately so that neither had to be concerned with constituents who would favor a philosophical fight to the death. (Gwyn, R. 2007) He began by appealing to Brown for a public show of unity which made sense to Brown who could see that their constant verbal abuse was not helping, even though publicly acceptable.

Macdonald's suggestion to Brown that he throw his support to Macdonald to be the First Prime Minister of Canada and concede his own, was just audacious enough to appeal to Brown. He listened carefully as MacDonald argued that with Brown's support their constituents would be unified through their mutual trust in both leaders. For this compromise MacDonald promised there would be laws which guaranteed permanent and fair representation for all constituents in every part of Canada. After careful deliberation Brown agreed.

MacDonald went on to become the first Prime Minister and Brown went back to being a prominent newspaper editor; both continued to work for the greater good of Canada. Both exhibited *extreme heroism* but if there was a greater *extreme hero* in this instance it had to be

Brown – the hero behind the hero who took heroism to higher ground - giving up personal aspirations of leading the country into nationhood, admitting that MacDonald with his gifts could do an even better job. The good of the nation was more important than his personal agenda.

Such heroism brought together two halves of Canada at a time when in the United States, North and South were about to be entangled in a terrible, costly Civil War which in some ways is still being fought. At another time and place, centuries later, there would come another extreme hero, writer and poet, Vaclav Havel who would emerge as the first democratically elected president of Czechoslovakia after 41 years without democracy, who would say "When a person tries to act in accordance with his [or her] conscience, when he tries to speak the truth, when he tries to behave like a citizen, even in conditions where citizenship is degraded, it won't necessarily lead anywhere, but it might…Even a purely moral act that has no hope of any immediate and visible effect can gradually and indirectly, over time, gain in political significance."(Havel, 2009) In other words, we show up, we bring what we have and the rest is history.

WORKS CITED

Chittister, J. (2009, July 28). *Sojourners.* Retrieved July 28, 2009, from Verse and Voice: www.sojo.net

Einstein, A. (2013, February 13). *Sojourners.* Retrieved February 13, 2013, from Verse and Voice: www.sojo.net

Gwyn, R. (2007). *"John A: The Man Who Made Use: The Life and Times of John A MacDonald, 1815-1867, Vol. I.* Toronto: Random House Canada.

Havel, V. (2009, May 9). *Sojourners.* Retrieved May 9, 2009, from Verse and Voice: www.sojo.net

CHAPTER 4

EXTREME HEROISM AND GENDER

Extreme Heroism and Women

There's evidence in ancient literature that heroism, generally speaking, has been attributed to women as well as men, off and on since before the Common Era...but while heroism was recognized in both women and men the attribution never held for long. Whenever gender equality DID catch on for relatively brief periods, it seemed to happen during times of relative peace and prosperity, but in times of war or conditions of poverty, women lost their status as heroes and their standing as equals. Judging by what we see today, the risks women take in the interest of saving other lives, including men, are as significant and frequent as the men.

Female heroes existed long before the first century, according the late Joseph Campbell. Their recognition he surmised was suppressed and delayed by the fact that male hero stories were told and repeated by men around tribal campfires while stories of female heroism were related in fairy-tales told to children at bed-time. The reason was simple said Campbell. "Women had little time for telling their own hero stories. They were too busy being heroes-behind-the-heroes to the men and other children in their life." (Campbell, 2008)

The domestic arena is where many women learn to behave heroically– giving birth, maintaining a home, parenting, nurturing and teaching – domestic activities which provide more than ample injustice and therefore opportunities for extreme heroism. Extreme heroism for women does not stop at the domestic margins. It spills over into neighborhoods, communities, churches, mosques, synagogues, offices where men also expend their energies.

When women moved beyond the domestic boundaries in more primitive societies, there were always males wanting to send them back. In every society there are women who refuse to go; women like Valerie Andre' in France who rose to the rank of first female General in the French Army in 1976, but not through the usual channels that men tend to follow. Valerie, in deciding where to apply her considerable gifts and talents, chose to become a brain surgeon and then learned to fly helicopters, before joining France's army.

She fought wars with medical and surgical weapons to save lives in the French Indonesian War which included Vietnam and Algiers. By 1962 she had flown 356 combat missions in bringing her healing skills to bear on countless battlefield casualties. (Osborne, 2008)

The cause of extreme female heroism over the centuries has been helped at times and hindered at others by many institutions, including those of religion. They were helped when Christians in the 3rd and 4th centuries began venerating Mary, mother of Jesus, as mother of God. This broke new ground for women and paved a way forward for women to expand their abilities beyond the home by portraying them as capable of holiness as any male.

Mary was undoubtedly a major influence in shaping Jesus' own understanding of heroism and she has been considered a patron saint of all women looking to exercise their considerable abilities. While the Catholic Church has done much to venerate women, there remains the optics that women are ineligible for the papacy and not entitled to names like priest and bishop which would signal gender equality.

Anthologies of women who rose to prominence in past, due in part to the encouragement of the Roman Catholic Church, were: Hildegard of Bingen (1098-1179); Mechthild of Magdeburg (1207-c. 1297?); Julian of Norwich (1342-c.1423); Catherine of Siena (1347-1380); Joan of Arc (1412-1431; Teresa of Avila (1515-1582); Ann Lee (1736-1784) and many others. (Cahill, 1996) The Protestant Church in its various forms added its influence to encouraging women after the 13th century: women like Sojourner Truth (1797-1883); Elizabeth Cady Stanton (1815-1902); Florence Nightingale (1820-1910); Eleanor Roosevelt (1884-1962). (Cahill, 1996)

While religious groups have always been in a position to defend a woman's right to live heroically beyond the domestic scene, they have also been known to gang up on women. All across the Middle East, even as we speak, men use religious influence to confine female heroism as narrowly as possible. It wasn't that long ago in Canada and the United States that women were similarly confined.

It was Elizabeth Cady Stanton who uttered a rallying cry with a just a hint of religious fervor to female heroes in the National American Woman Suffrage Association in 1890, saying to women: "The moment we begin to fear the opinions of others and hesitate to tell the truth that is in us, and from motives of policy are silent when we should speak, the divine floods of light and life flow no longer in our souls." (Stanton, 2012) In other words, extreme heroism like any other gift, can be weakened, atrophied and even buried, if not used.

50 years ago, without a lot of fanfare, most mainline Protestant churches in North America began behaving heroically toward women… encouraging women to take up leadership roles within the church… top leadership roles…clergy, pastors, bishops, etc., by asking them to consider professional ministry as vocation. It was dawning on the church in the 1960s that having men as the only visible leaders in the pulpit was not helping women or men. Poor optics perpetuate old stereotypes.

So it was the 1960s women when began appearing in pulpits for the first time; I remember coming back from military service in South Korea, going to a church on Sunday morning, seeing with my own eyes, my first clergywoman I had ever seen in the pulpit. Until then, most Canadians and Americans had never seen female ministers wearing clergy shirts or clerical robes or presiding over holy-communion. By the 1970s female enrollment in Protestant seminaries had jumped to over 30 percent; more and more women were being called as solo ministers.

Men entering seminary during that time became the first recipients and beneficiaries of extreme heroism as practiced by their female colleagues. Women in Protestant seminaries continue now into the 21st century at or near 50 percent as solo ministers in small churches and chief executives in larger churches. While they may not all be aware of their contribution, women have now helped five generations of North Americans visualize the extreme heroism in women.

Like victims of racial prejudice, women have been gender victims of hero bias for centuries. Those aware of this injustice have had good reasons to be angry and even hostile toward men, yet women have learned from African-Americans to think of men as those who have much to gain from the emancipation of women, just as white Americans have much to gain through the emancipation of black Americans.

Of course domestic heroism by women is both acceptable and legendary; children, spouses, mothers, teachers and others, when asked to list the heroes in their lives almost always list mothers, grandmothers, aunts or sisters. Most everyone can think of a female educator or a female mentor who fought for them against the injustices that imperiled their lives growing up. The list began to grow in the late 1800s and early 1900s when women began moving beyond their families in resisting injustice from unlicensed liquor manufacture, child slavery, prostitution, bullying in schools and neighborhood, inadequate health care, along with being denied the right to vote or own property.

The expansion of female heroism still has much room for growth in the world wherever men still dominate – in business, in politics and in nations where female heroism is still confined to the domestic situations. Bottom line…extreme heroism is not the sole domain of men. Boundaries against female heroism wherever imposed are arbitrary and inappropriate. Extreme heroism is a female and male quality.

Teen-Age Girl Heroes in Iowa

Along the border between Iowa and Illinois where Amtrak passenger trains cross the Mississippi River there's an area known as the Quad Cities of Davenport, Moline-East Moline, Rock Island and Bittendorf.

It is the home of a group of teenage girls known as the Spartan Sparkles who were first noticed and honored as heroes by television host Oprah Winfrey. At the time they were teenage girls attending Sparta High School in a place called Pleasant Valley, Iowa.

The name Sparta lends a bit of irony to the story since Sparta is a name of an ancient Greek city that was considered the home of many male super-heroes. At first glance the Spartan Sparkles seemed like many other cheer leading teams who gather on Friday and Saturday nights during the school year to lead others in cheers, waving pom-poms and rooting for their respective sports teams. The word 'hero' does not immediately come to mind in just hearing the name 'cheer leaders'.

These girls were that and *more.* They intentionally recruited girls with disabilities like autism and Down's syndrome for their cheer-leading team.

It all began when two teenage girls sensed the injustice of girls with disabilities never considered for cheer-leading because people have a collective obsession with physical symmetry in its females and males which leads to great social harm and hurt. Guided by remarkable good will and old-fashioned extreme heroism the Spartan Sparkles put their lives on the line after two girls, Sarah C and Sarah H, witnessed young athletes at the World Special Olympics and came home wanting for the good witnessed in the world to be extended to girls in their home town. They talked to their coach who supported them in living out their vision (Spartan Sparkles, 2010).

In order that this book be usable as a teaching tool, there is at the conclusion of each story/illustration an analysis which identifies (1) injustice motivating the hero to act and (2) evidence that responses were guided by indiscourageable good will for all involved. For example: **(1) Injustice like this toward physical appearance is made worse by being entrenched in school settings and tolerated by authorities. (2) Indiscourageable good will toward victims and uninformed perpetrators is essential to restoring justice, the likes of which many people have never seen until they visit a school like this.**

Extreme Female Heroes Emerge in North Texas

Four years after the Sparkles appeared on national television other female heroes began emerging around the U.S. There was a story from a high school in Grand Prairie, Texas, where two candidates for the year's homecoming queen got wind of a cruel prank being imposed on a classmate. The friend's natural sweetness and innocence became a target for someone reporting falsely that the friend had been nominated for homecoming queen.

Two girls, Anahi Alvarez and Naomi Martinez, actual nominees for homecoming queen, discovered this injustice and vowed to each other that if either of them were elected as homecoming queen they would pass their crown to their innocent victimized classmate.

It happened. One of them was elected and before the award was to be given at half-time at a football game, Alvarez and Martinez had told the principal Lorimer Arendse their intentions. He enthusiastically supported the young women in their decision and said later that it was probably the greatest moment he had ever experienced as a principal. On cue, having escorted Lillian and others onto the field for crowning, Arendse awarded Lillian Skinner the crown for homecoming queen. (Russell, 2014)

In order that this book be usable as a teaching tool, there is at the conclusion of each story/illustration an analysis which identifies (1) injustice motivating the hero to act and (2) evidence that responses were guided by indiscourageable good will for all involved. For example: **(1) Injustice in school settings toward innocence itself is a cruel form of bullying. Not everyone perceives innocence as a weakness, but some adolescent youth do. They respond accordingly. (2) Responding to this kind of injustice can only be responded to with indiscourageable good will. The response itself cannot be perceived as retaliation. These two girls risked losing their own popularity.**

Extreme Female Hero in Australia/New Zealand - Jessica Watson

Sixteen-year-old Jessica Watson of Australia/New Zealand concluded a solo sail (23,000 nautical miles) around the world in the early afternoon of May 15, 2010. She captured the attention of the world after sweeping the people of her two homelands off their feet as she sailed into Sidney Harbor. The exuberance and outpouring of enthusiasm over her accomplishment is something which often happens when acts are truly heroic – it's because of the way everyone feels about the event – it arouses within us something called joy in which we feel good about ourselves, good about everyone else and if we profess a belief in God or a Higher Power we probably feel good about God/our Higher Power too.

Jessica's act touched the hearts of women and girls all over the planet because she said, "I hated being judged by my appearance and other people's expectations of what a little girl is capable of." (Lulham, 2010) When the Lord Mayor of Sydney, Clover Moore, addressed an adoring crowd on the day of Jessica's return, she proclaimed Jessica's accomplishment "an occasion for all Australians and New Zealanders to stand taller" [stand taller…code words for joy] - women and girls, men and boys, all New Zealanders and Australians standing taller because one person had sensed an injustice, responded to it with good will and established a new measure of justice that produced joy.

In order that this book be usable as a teaching tool, there is at the conclusion of each story/illustration an analysis which identifies (1) injustice motivating the hero to act and (2) evidence that responses were guided by indiscourageable good will for all involved. For example: **(1) The injustice of prejudice against a young female who can't possibly be expected to sail around the world alone is obvious. (2) Her response was to risk all of her lives (physical, emotional, mental and spiritual) and show herself capable of doing in four different ways, simultaneously, what they said teenage girls couldn't possibly do.**

Tamako Nakagawa Kubota Extreme Hero of Hiroshima and Lethbridge

She lived at least 3 lives: a life in Japan before the atomic bombs were dropped on Japan, August 6, 1945; a life in Japan after the atomic bomb; and a life in Lethbridge, Alberta, Canada after she married "Taki" Kubota. From the first part of her life we know that Tamako was an elementary school teacher in a village just a short walk south of the Japanese metropolis of Hiroshima. She and her teacher colleagues were busily welcoming students back to school that morning...the last day of the first part of her life.

She remembered one of the other teachers calling out to her to "Look up!" High in the sky above was a solitary airplane which she had no way of knowing was a B-29 bomber named the Enola Gay flying quietly high above, at least from their perspective. "Moments later," Tamako said, "a strong flash of light blinded me, and next a big bang shook the earth. I instinctively covered my exposed arms with my hands. Then strong gusts of wind started hitting us." (Kubota, 1986)

"We looked in the direction of the noise and saw the cloud that we know now as a mushroom cloud. The grey, white, and black colored cloud made of many round pillars, which rose in the sky...Its tip was a red fireball." Something awful had to have happened, so Tamako and the other teachers started sending children home. "It was then that large black rain drops began to fall. The river turned black. About an hour later we saw...many victims of the bombing walking toward our school, coming from Hiroshima. Many...were barefooted.*"

**[the explosion having lifted them out of their shoes.]*

"A woman with a baby was crying as she walked along...a baby that was not hers but a neighbor's with whom she had been talking moments before the bomb detonated. The mother had simply said, "Here, hold my baby for a moment!" She went inside and disappeared as her house collapsed from the blast…such a sad sight. Many came and continued on, trudging, stumbling down the road. One after another, all day long they came."

The third part of Tamako's life began with an introduction to the man whom she would marry...a man nicknamed 'Taki'...who would bring her to Canada to be his wife. They would make their home in Lethbridge, Alberta, where Tamako would become a respected member of the Japanese-Canadian community. In later years, when August 6 was set aside by the United Nations as World Peace Day, Tamako got involved and every year for many years told her story to peace advocates who gathered in Lethbridge for the annual observance.

Her story-telling became the central feature of her heroic response to the injustice she and countless others endured as victims of war. She told her story year after year after year ...not with anger toward the military leaders of Japan nor the United States but with tones of grace and good will. She died peacefully in 2012 at age 98, surrounded by the family of her third life*.

> *(A copy of Tamako's annual speech was supplied for the writing of this book by her granddaughter, Lonnie Dee [Kubota] Antal, who later forwarded a letter of permission from her father and Tamako's Step-Son, Richard Kubota on behalf of the Kubota family, March, 2015)

It was United Nations Secretary-General Ban Ki-Moon whose words were meant for millions and millions of people around the world like Tamako Nakagawa Kubota when he said in 2010, "Together, we are on a journey from ground zero to Global Zero – a world free of weapons of mass destruction...Let us realize our dream of a world free of nuclear weapons so that our children and all succeeding generations can live in freedom, security, and peace." (Sojourners, 2010)

Two days earlier it was reported by Sojourners Daily Digest, "Survivors of the atomic bombings of Hiroshima and Nagasaki are welcoming a decision by the United States to send its first ever delegation to a ceremony marking the anniversary of the attacks, but they are asking for something they aren't likely to get – an apology." People to this day still have trouble responding to grave injustice with anything less than revenge (Sojourners, 2010). The injustice of Nagasaki and Hiroshima and that of Japan's military against the United States, so huge, will require many, many acts of good will, grace, forgiveness, kindness and compassion from people like Tamako Kubota before it will become right and just again.

It was Franklin Delano Roosevelt, President of the U.S. during most of World War II, who said, "I have seen war. I have seen war on land and sea…I have seen the dead in the mud. I have seen cities destroyed…I have seen children starving. I have seen the agony of mothers and wives. I hate war." (Sojourners, 2009)

He spoke as one, who, like Tamako, had seen, tasted, smelled and heard the awfulness of war up close and knew it to be dreadful beyond words. The sight provoked in both a humble President and a humble Japanese-Canadian school teacher, an aversion to war and affinity for good will for all.

In order that this book be usable as a teaching tool, there is at the conclusion of each story/illustration an analysis which identifies (1) injustice motivating the hero to act and (2) evidence that responses were guided by indiscourageable good will for all involved. For example: **(1) War is what nations do when they are trying to trump one injustice with another. The Injustice of war against individuals is impossible to measure but is amplified when leaders hurry to wage it. (2) The response of one victim multiplied perhaps a million times is a good beginning to making things right again.**

Reverend Connie –Extreme Hero of the Plains

It was Christmas Day morning…barely daylight when the telephone rang. The Reverend Constance, known to her parishioners as Connie, groped for the phone in the dark as she lifted one eye-lid to check the time. Putting on her office voice she tried to sound reasonably alert. "This is Pastor Connie."

When the female voice on the other end identified herself as an Emergency Room Charge Nurse at a hospital thirty miles away, apologizing for calling at such an early hour, Connie eyes widened and she sat up. "I'm calling on behalf of one of your church members," the nurse said, "whose son just died." Connie turned on the lamp on her bedside table and reached for a pen which she kept there.

She stared at her own hand, disbelieving the name flowing out of her pen - the name of a young man whose family she knew well. His father and mother had been like a brother and sister, Connie never had. They would have been close friends had they not been parishoners.

"Died?" "Oh Dear God"

"Yes. His pickup truck rolled over on Highway 40. He was almost home when it happened. He died here soon after the ambulance arrived."

"Please tell the family I'm on my way! I'll be there in about thirty minutes!"

Connie hung up the phone and turned to find Tom, who had been listening to her side of the conversation, already getting dressed and loading his pockets with change, car keys and wallet. Connie hurriedly threw on a bulky sweatshirt over her clergy-shirt and jeans as the two of them rushed to the garage and their car. They drove out into the early darkness in silence with the deep blue lights of the dashboard lighting their faces.

About ten miles out of town, they slowed as they came to the wreckage still strewn along the highway. Two highway patrol cars with flashing lights and the county coroner were out beside the highway in the dim morning light measuring and taking notes. The coroner whom Connie knew well, looked up and waved as their car slowed.

"Bobby was so proud of his truck," Connie thought as the car eased slowly past and sped up again, "It had been a symbol to his arrival at adulthood...joining ranks with his Dad and the other ranchers. As they moved past the tragic sight of Bobby's scattered belongings, truck upside down, Connie's thoughts turned to the children she and Tom had decided not to have...so glad that those imaginary children would not be deprived of a normal Christmas morning, opening presents around the tree and then felt guilty for thinking that.

Her thoughts returned to what lay ahead for her as the car picked up speed and the words she might be called upon to say at the hospital, began to percolate through her thoughts. She frightened herself with images of the two doting parents for whom this son was everything…a symbol of their hope for the future. She also knew that this visit to the hospital would only be the first of what would be dozens and dozens of emotionally, spiritually, intellectually hazardous, risky occasions that would be repeated for many days and even weeks.

Death has a strange effect on people. Relationships that are normally safe and desirable prior to death are rendered risky by death. People who normally know no boundaries in a rural community suddenly keep their distance, hesitant to go near the grief-stricken. Clergy like Connie are among the few first responders who arrive to fill that space and begin the long trek forward toward new life and new justice.

As Tom pulled into the hospital parking lot the sun was still just below the horizon. The hospital evening lights were still on, lining the long circular driveway. As they drove in and parked, Connie said another prayer, hugged Tom and braced for initial contact.

Their footsteps echoed as they walked quickly down the gleaming hallway, recently buffed, toward the emergency room. The charge-nurse recognized Pastor Connie and asked her to follow to a room marked "No Admittance – Authorized Personnel Only". She pushed the big "Open" button and the doors yielded.

The poor, poor parents were standing there in the center of an intensely lit room beside an operating table still holding the body of their son. They were clutching each other in their night clothes, faces ashen, stained with dried tears, eyes hollow with shock. "Would all of Connie's hero-training be enough…this time?"

Connie wasn't using the words hero or hero-school in her thoughts. If she had, she too might have asked if all her seminary training would be enough. It would be, but as an older minister/hero friend had once told her, "You are about to need every bit of training you ever received and then some."

You show up. You bring what you have. You trust deeply in the divine more…that thing they called "then some".

Do not think that this will be the worst of it or the end of it or the most dangerous. Not so. There will be much more ahead in the way of emotional, spiritual risk and danger lurking along the way as you lead others through times like these. It's one of the reasons that churches, synagogues, mosques and other centers of learning and comfort are so important.

There were contacts similar to those with the parents, repeated again and again as siblings of the deceased began to arrive...each gathering and embracing their parents...each arrival hazardous...each needing comfort and requiring the right words, a touch or just a presence. As more siblings and friends arrive the parents begin to feel stronger and better able to respond to their other children. There will come the day of the funeral with literally thousands of people from a very theologically diverse religious community who will come to give something of themselves to the bereaved yet ready with harsh criticism for the minister and family if they hear or see something which offends.

At this point the entire gathered community needs words and touch which comfort and reassure. Conversations with God, called prayer, will be needed so that everyone hears an appeal to their Higher Power for justice. All these things take place as it were, on the edge of an emotional, spiritual, intellectual precipice...a tight-rope...over a coffin, a waiting empty grave and an uncertain future.

The secular world knows very little about this aspect of heroism which the religious world calls ministry, discipleship, priesthood, even sainthood...which is heroism-become-extreme. In truth, it is non-stop extreme heroism, risky, dangerous, and best guided by indiscourageable good will for all.

In order that this book be usable as a teaching tool, there is at the conclusion of each story/illustration an analysis which identifies (1) injustice motivating the hero to act and (2) evidence that responses were guided by indiscourageable good will for all involved. For example: **(1) The Injustice of a child's death is one of the greater injustices known. To have it happen on a special day like Christmas magnifies the injustice. Parents and family live with that injustice for the rest of their lives. (2) Responding to this injustice can only be guided by indiscourageable good will to the Creator, one another and even the deceased.**

Extreme Heroes as Male

I saw no need here for an equal number of male examples of extreme heroism to be told here because it's already easy for us to think of men as heroes although that has often meant men at war, men in law enforcement, men in search and rescue, men as emergency medical responders, etc. Men deserve recognition for their extreme heroism as much as anyone, but as Angela Y. Davis put it, "No march, movement, or agenda that defines manhood in the narrowest terms and seeks to make women lesser partners in this quest for equality can be considered a positive step." Men should try their hand at extreme heroism by becoming primary advocates and supporters for women wherever they can, no less than Susan B. Anthony who wrote, "I pray every single second of my life, not on my knees, but with my work. My prayer is to lift woman to equality with man." (Anthony, 2011)

WORKS CITED

Anthony, S. B. (2011). *Sojourners.* Retrieved from Verse and Voice: www.sojo.net

Cahill, S. (1996). *Wise Women.* New York, N.Y.: W. W. Norton & Company, Inc.

Campbell, J. (2008). *The Hero With A Thousand Faces.* Novato, California: New World Library.

Davis, A. Y. (2014, Octboer 30). *Sojourners.* Retrieved October 30, 2014, from Verse & Voice: www.sojo.net

Kubota, T. N. (1986). Lethbridge, Alberta, Canada.

Lulham, A. (2010, May 14). *Daily Telegraph Sydney Australia.* Retrieved May 14, 2010, from www.dailytelegraph.com.au

Osborne, L. B. (2008). Editor. *Women Who Dare.* Petaluma, California, USA: Library of Congress.

Russell, B. (2014). *Homecoming Queen.* New York: NBC Evening News.

Sojourners. (2009, August 4). Retrieved August 4, 2009, from Verse & Voice: www.sojo.net

Sojourners. (2010, August 6). Retrieved August 6, 2010, from Verse & Voice: www.sojo.net

Sojourners. (2010, Augist 5). Retrieved August 5, 2010, from Daily Digest: www.sojo.net

Spartan Sparkles. (2010, March-April). *Clallam Connection, Volume 2, Issue 2.* U.S.: Clallam County.

Stanton, E. C. (2012, June 5). *Sojourners.* Retrieved June 5, 2012, from Verse & Voice: www.sojo.net

CHAPTER 5

EXTREME HEROISM AND AGE

The Myth That the Very Young and the Very Old Can't Be Heroes

In a perfect world there would be complete awareness of extreme heroism along with the understanding that this form of heroism is innate to the human condition – normal - part of our DNA if you will. In a perfect world we would be inclined to anticipate extreme heroism in each other and look for signs of it soon after birth because we know it's capable of flourishing very early in childhood. We would also understand that so long as there's nothing to interfere with it, extreme heroism will continue to mature through adulthood and beyond into our centenarian years.

But in the real world the whole spectrum of heroism is thought to be the domain of our strong years. Children and youth are not expected to behave heroically even for a moment nor is anything expected of the elderly so we are surprised when it happens. The real world of course is wrong about this aspect of heroism and about age.

According to Mairead Maguire Corrigan, "Every day there are people in our world that do absolutely amazing things. People of all ages are very capable of doing tremendous, courageous things in spite of their fear." (Maguire)

Applauding Extreme Heroism When It Appears in the Very Young

The key to extreme heroism at any age is something residing deep within us. Our ability to detect injustice...to know when something is unfair or wrong...begins soon after birth. I've mentioned the following story before but mention it again in order say that wherever our sensitivity to injustice resides, the impulse toward extreme heroism also resides: A young mother writing in her annual Christmas letter to the larger family reflects on a 3-year-old son's emergent behavior during the year: "He really lets us know now when he thinks a family rule has been violated or a family promise has been broken. He holds us accountable and won't let us get away with anything that seems unfair."

It is also interesting to see how young children already understand and recognize heroism when they hear it in a story or see it in the behavior of others. I recently watched a new movie with three of my grandchildren, a movie starring well known stand-up comics from television's *Saturday Night Live.* The movie was about juvenile behavior in adults and like most movies it had its share of heroes who were struggling to make good decisions.

Afterward, at a restaurant, with everyone munching on a snack before starting the drive home, the children – aged 13, 10 and 4 - were asked "What did you think was the important part of the movie?" There was the usual rolling of the eyes and the "I don't know" answers, but when asked "Who was the hero in this movie?" all three children immediately voiced an opinion and were absolutely unanimous in nominating one of the actors as the greater hero. When asked, "What made her the hero?" Without prompting they all had correct answers.

Extremely Heroic at Age Eleven

An 11-year-old boy with advanced leukemia was arriving in a major city with his parents. They were on their way to a children's hospital several miles from the city center and the boy was seated in the backseat of his parent's car, gazing out the window as it slowed for heavy rush-hour traffic. Suddenly he sat upright at seeing homeless people living in cardboard boxes beneath a freeway overpass.

Neither the child's ailment nor his young age, kept him from perceiving the injustice of homelessness in an otherwise prosperous city. The sight only adds to the pain the boy is already suffering and by the time they reach the hospital he is feeling faint but asking his parents, "Please. Isn't there something we can do for these people?" The parents had learned that things like this upset their son, so they promised to talk about his question which they did later with a hospital admission team.

The hospital staff responded with genuine concern as they routinely do with sick children, believing that by taking such concerns seriously they might discover a key to defeating a child's disease. In time and in this case, the staff members were able to help the child's parents organize a day for sending meals, warm blankets, coats and clean clothing to those seen under the overpass. Word even went out to the local media who respond to the human interest aspect of the appeal; the general public responds by contributing generously to television appeals.

Even the homeless, in hearing the story, respond favorably. Normally known for their fierce independence and contempt for the dole they make an exception and accept the gifts in the child's name. The child has reacted heroically to the injustice he sees without prompting.

In order that this book be usable as a teaching tool, there is at the conclusion of each story/illustration an analysis which identifies (1) injustice motivating the hero to act and (2) evidence that responses were guided by indiscourageable good will for all involved. For example: **(1) Disease is an injustice. Even though sick, the child could still see the injustice of people living in cardboard boxes in the midst of a wealthy city. (2) The medical profession is itself a collection of heroic responses to disease with intent to restore health/justice. The child responds to this injustice in typical fashion. The parents and the hospital staff respond to the injustice of a child suffering at the sight of another person's suffering. Imagine the indiscourageable good will of the parents and hospital staff responding to the child's sensitivities and the poor beneath the overpass.**

There are those who maintain that helping to heal others also heals the healers. The things that happened in that hospital and beyond it, on behalf of this child, are worth doing. However, in this case, their efforts will come too late but they do bring a small measure of solace, to both the boy and to the homeless. He dies of leukemia but not before improving the lives of others.

Theologian Dorothee Soelle in paraphrasing her analysis of the Hebrew Book of Job (Holy Bible, The New Revised Standard Version, 1997) said "In a religion that is intent on the self, there can be no real encounter between God and the human being. Our own healing and betterment is inseparable from the healing and betterment of others." Soelle points to the way "Job connects his fate to that of other innocent sufferers and discovers his sisters and brothers whose land had been stolen, their animals impounded, their clothing and shelter taken away. He himself changes as he relates the impoverishment of the poor and their innocent suffering to his own situation."

"Such siding with the poor does not solve his own problem; it does not end his ill fortunes...but it does give him peace which is the beginning place for healing as he concludes that God is the father of all victims of injustice, that their situation will not remain as it is, and that the historical losers in the global economy are not forgotten, superfluous beings that can be ignored." Both this child's response to injustice and Job's response to injustice - were acts of extreme heroism. Their responses may not have ended their ill fortune but they set in motion waves of justice that are still washing ashore long after they have departed from this life. While heroism becomes evident in most of us soon after birth, the real challenge is keeping this heroic impulse alive...not letting it be eroded by cynicism or buried by the prejudice of adulthood.

Extreme Teen Heroism in a Dollar Store

We can learn to respond to injustice using extreme heroism wherever and whenever the opportunity arises. Trust that the instincts are there whether we are religious or non-religious.

A 13-year-old girl visiting her grandparents had just stopped into the local Dollar Store to do some shopping. As she waited in line at the cash register to pay for her purchases, she happened to stand behind a little boy and his grandfather doing the same thing. The little boy, about 8-years-old, was making a purchase with his own money but clearly didn't have enough money to finish paying for it; short 62 cents.

His grandfather was embarrassed to say that he couldn't help and so it looked bad for the little boy, but the girl was so moved by the injustice she saw playing out in front of her that she gave the boy three of her own quarters to cover the cost and told him to keep the change. The little boy and grandfather responded gratefully.

A seed sown, planted by a 13-year-old girl…a story that her mother urged her daughter to retell that evening around the family dinner table. While she might not get to see what her deed might produce she can count on it producing something good that someday someone else will see.

In order that this book be usable as a teaching tool, there is at the conclusion of each story/illustration an analysis which identifies (1) injustice motivating the hero to act and (2) evidence that responses were guided by indiscourageable good will for all involved. For example: **(1) The injustice of 'not having enough to meet our obligations' whether a small purchase or the mortgage payment, (2) calls upon a 13-year-old to respond with the resources she has at her disposal. She has to risk rejection from the boy and/or his grandfather or scolding from the cashier for holding up the line or the customer standing in line behind her.**

Extreme Boy Hero on the Big Yellow Bus

Billy was a shy farm boy who rode a big yellow bus to school every day - nineteen miles, one way, into the city – to a learning island set in a sea of leafy green sugar beets, alfalfa, oats, beans, potatoes, peas, tomatoes and just about every other vegetable found on a farm or a grocery store. Thurston Meadows Elementary was the name of this island - a brand new school built by the school board on the south edge of town to accommodate rural children from the southern part of the county. Billy was nine years old, a student in the third grade.

Every other day was mathematics day, first hour after lunch - Monday, Wednesday and Friday - taught by Miss Stone. Miss Stone maintained a very severe appearance…her white hair always tied tightly in a bun. She matched this look with a style of teaching that she believed the best tool for prying open the minds of nine-year-olds - intimidation.

From day-one Billy lived in dread of mathematics class. To Miss Stone's credit, her methods DID seem to lead to competency in two things for Billy: *numbers*…and…*prayer*. At home in the evenings, he would stare at the numbers he was trying to understand until they began to swim across the page all the while he was praying to God for protection from Miss Stone.

On the mornings of math class he prayed on the bus on its way to the school and during every free moment of the other classes. The funny thing is that no one had taught him to pray. Whether his parents prayed or not, Bill didn't know. He never saw it being done. No one instructed him. It was instinctive…a primitive response that would eventually probably prove effective for Billy in ways he would never understand.

Miss Stone's customary routine was to march the children to the chalk board at the front of the room to solve math problems. She would walk up and down behind them patting a long slender stick in her left hand with which she would suddenly and dramatically point to a math problem, ask questions of a trembling student, and then hit them in the back of the head with her open palm if they couldn't fathom the correct answer. By today's teaching standards she might have been dismissed for such a teaching style.

To Billy it seemed that he got preferential treatment in the sense that when HE failed to comprehend a problem, Miss Stone hit him so hard his head literally bounced off the chalk board! Billy's prayers changed from *protect me* to *help me understand and get the answer before she hits me again*! Perhaps as an answer to his prayer, Billy began to learn.

More and more often and to his own surprise he would come up with the correct answer. The hits from behind became less frequent, but did not stop entirely. Still, it was a big improvement.

It would be a lie to say that Miss Stone was Billy's favorite teacher, but she was one of the most memorable. Perhaps Miss Stone really did love children but her love was hard, like stone…too difficult for young Billy to detect. He was sure that she liked him the least of all the children. If Billy had already been a deeply traumatized child, Miss Stone could have pushed the trauma to a psychotic break.

Billy never told his parents about Miss Stone. He never complained about her to them or any of the other students – these were times when teachers ruled with an iron hand. It would appear that his response to this classroom injustice was passive – a do-nothing response - if we didn't already know that his whole life was a response through constant, intense prayer and study.

To his credit it never occurred to him to respond with violence. He never got sick in order to stay home from school. The only thing he did was pray for 'help' from a higher power as nine-year olds understand higher power.

Prayer in the face of injustice qualifies as an initial and crucially important heroic response to injustice – not a bad response even for adults. Sometimes it is the only immediate response available to those being victimized, and a far better response than doing nothing or responding violently.

In order that this book be usable as a teaching tool, there is at the conclusion of each story/illustration an analysis which identifies (1) injustice motivating the hero to act and (2) evidence that responses were guided by indiscourageable good will for all involved. For example: **(1) Injustice in classroom settings seems to have been common to both public and church-sponsored schools. (2) Billy's response if not good will was certainly respectful. Respect, if it can be mustered, is a good response toward abusive authority when down deep it wants to teach well.**

Yes. There Is Such a Thing as Extreme Elder Heroism

Yes, of course; sensitivities to injustice do not wane just because we're older…if anything, they become stronger…not only to the injustices of growing older, but to the varieties of injustice being imposed on others. It's our ABILITY to respond to injustice that changes as we grow older...especially the things that were easy to do when we were young because such was our strength. In youth we have one set of tools for responding to injustice, but we will discover and hone additional skills for responding in our middle age and then again in old age.

If all goes well as we continue to age we discover and develop those rudimentary skills we've always had but never learned to utilize fully. But what we often see are people arriving at old age firmly believing there was one way and one way only for responding injustice. They turn away from injustice because they can't do the things they once did. They hear reports of injustice but make no response because they don't believe there's anything they can do that would make a difference.

As our early strengths wane and incomes become fixed we see ourselves as 'washed up' with nothing more we can contribute, but the truth is that as long as we can think and arrange words together in sentences and as long as we still have a personal presence and a voice in some form, we can continue to function as extreme heroes right up to our last breath on this earth. That's the nature of extreme heroism...it's always there and ready to define who we are.

An Eighty-Five Year Old Extreme Hero

Art was 43 and to him his life was all but over. His marriage of two decades had just ended in divorce and he found himself a single parent with four children...two in older elementary grade school and two in high school. He supposed it could be worse...she could have taken the children with her...but it was hard for him to remember this on that morning in late August when he walked into a department store to buy back-to-school clothes and realized, as he stood looking at children's underwear, that he didn't have clue as to his children's clothing sizes.

A typical married male of his generation he had abdicated almost all specific knowledge of his children's physical characteristics. He had never cooked for his children before and now he had a very steep learning curve in terms of their likes and dislikes of food. He felt badly...even guilty that he didn't know such things.

He had just resigned as a minister of a suburban church because he realized what a terrible husband he had been and now he was seeing what a terrible father he had been. In the weeks preceding he had found a job at a counseling institution and was trying to adjust to the resulting changes in his professional routine. Things he used to do every day in the parish he could no longer use as a professional counselor so now he was developing listening and counseling skills to bring to bear on the injustice counselees were facing in their lives.

Into this circumstance one day there came a very old extreme hero whom some might have called an angel. The office phone rang and the receptionist told Art, "There's a long distance call for you from a Fred Jamieson in Toronto." Art thought to himself, "I don't know any Fred Jamieson or anyone in Toronto."

Turns out it was a denominational executive from the national church Art had served, but he wasn't just any denominational executive. Fred, he would soon learn, was 84 years old and retired almost 20 years. He said over the phone, "I am planning a trip out your way and expect to be in your city next Friday. I'll take a cab from the airport and should be at your office by 10:30AM. Will that work for you?"

Before hanging up, Fred explained that he had been called out of retirement to serve temporarily as Moderator of the denomination and was now tending to pastoral needs among the denomination's leadership. Art said of Fred's plans, "Of course…that will work perfectly. I just happen to have that time open on my calendar." He penciled the appointment in as his thoughts returned to the peculiar fact that this man was 84 years old, the same age as both of Art's grandfathers.

Art was waiting in the lobby the day Fred arrived. He was even more stunned by how fragile and frail the older man looked and yet here he was. Art cringed a bit as he watched Fred struggle to climb the steep flight of stairs with a cane in one hand and by pulling himself up the stairs with the other hand, one step at a time.*

*This being the days before the handicapped had been recognized and before builders started developing easier access.)

Later, as he reflected on that day, Art would say "I was standing there at the head of those steep steps, watching an *extreme hero* struggling to enter my world and my particular set of injustices, one painful step at a time in order to offer his presence, comfort, reassurance and vision for the future. Art was aware of the warmth in Fred's hand as he reached the summit and the kindness in his eyes. They walked slowly together down the carpeted hallway and entered Art's office.

Fred removed his coat, draped it over a chair, removed his cap and scarf (it was winter) and sat down, hooking his cane over the arm of the chair. They talked about the injustice in Art's life, who was quick to confess that he had caused a lot of injustice himself, that he had been a perpetrator as well as victim. Fred acknowledged Art's confession and they talked about those things for several minutes before Fred changed the subject and turned to ask about Art's children…how they were doing with the divorce.

In the course of their conversation Fred had the audacity to suggest that Art might want to remarry one day. It sure didn't seem likely to Art, but he appreciated the sentiment and references to a future he wasn't always sure he would have. Then this old and fragile hero praised Art for his work in the church…which Art could barely listen to as he looked back seeing only failure…yet Fred insisted on talking about the good Art had done, the lives he had saved and how much he meant to others.

An hour later, Fred labored slowly to stand and started putting on his scarf, cap and coat. He picked up his cane and they walked to the stairs. Art stepped alongside Fred as he let himself down the staircase to where a cab was waiting for Fred outside at the curb.

"So where you off to now?" Art asked cheerily, thinking that the Temporary Moderator of the National Church would surely have other appointments around the city. "Actually" he said, "I'm on my way back to the airport; my flight back to Toronto leaves about 3." Art was astounded. Two thousand miles was a long pastoral call! He climbed slowly back up the stairs, walked to his office and sat down to think about the implications of what Fred had just said…and done.

The man had traveled all the way across the continent to be present to someone whom he had never met. "He didn't know me from Adam" Art thought to himself "yet he traveled all that way just to be with the likes of me." In time Fred would become in Art's mind a very old extreme hero who came to reassure, reaffirm, speak well of the past and of the future, yet a man whom he would never see again, leaving Art with the possibility that he still had worth.

In order that this book be usable as a teaching tool, there is at the conclusion of each story/illustration an analysis which identifies (1) injustice motivating the hero to act and (2) evidence that responses were guided by indiscourageable good will for all involved. **(1) The injustice of divorce, personal and professional failure, (2) responded to by a man who ought NOT to have anything to respond with, because of his age, yet he does. He brings what he has...himself, 84 years of experience about life and goodness, compassion, kindness, optimism, faith in a higher power and indiscourageable good will.**

An Extreme Elderly Hero Between Floors

Soon after moving into the assisted-care facility Paul remembered standing on the balcony of his unit and seeing an elderly couple on the lawn below him starting out for what looked like their regular evening walk. He watched them until they disappeared into the distance and then returned to reading his book. It was over a year later that he saw them again, this time they were inside the building where they all lived.

On this occasion Paul was on the elevator riding up from the parking garage when the couple entered from the ground floor for a brief ride to the 2nd. A year later, with Paul on the elevator again, riding up from the parking garage as before when the same man got on at the ground floor, alone. He greeted Paul with a surprisingly hearty greeting given that they so seldom saw each other and after three years still didn't know each other's names.

"How are things with you?" was a question the man had never asked in their other encounters. Paul answered politely and truthfully, "Very well, thank you." then followed with "How are things with you?"

Staring straight ahead the man answered in a soft voice, "My wife just died. I'm going to be moving away to live with my son." Paul didn't hesitate to respond with genuine heart-felt concern. With the man still looking straight ahead Paul reached up (the other man was very tall) to lay his left hand on the man's right shoulder saying, "I'm so very sorry" and before Paul could say more the elevator doors opened on the 2nd floor, the man got off without looking back nor replying further. The doors closed behind him without another word or a glance or a wave.

Paul's opportunity for an act of extreme heroism lasted only 30 seconds and fortunately he filled those 30 seconds with something valuable; his presence, kindness, a touch and comforting words. A few days later it was the same man's adult sons who were seen loading their father's belongings onto a moving truck.

Looking back on this event Paul realized that maybe this man had been an extreme hero too…that perhaps this had been an example of double-heroism because the other man was a victim of injustice. The death was that of his wife. He responded to that injustice by informing Paul as to his circumstances, bravely sending words across the divide between them that began with, "How are things with you?"

Responding to the injustice of his wife's death and the injustice of being alone again, the unnamed stranger had responded to his own need for connection by informing another of his state of being. There was great risk in saying anything but he took the risk and overrode his need to be alone in his suffering. Of course there was risk also for Paul in making any kind of response, but the words shaped by good will came quickly and for 30 seconds, between floors, it filled the gap.

Perhaps seeds were planted so that life could begin again. The opportunities for investing extreme heroism sometimes can be so brief as to take our breath away. As Vietnamese Zen Buddhist Thich Nhat Hanh wrote, "In everyone there is the capacity to wake up, to understand, and to love." (Hanh, 2012) He didn't say just how quickly the wakeup call could come and go.

> In order that this book be usable as a teaching tool, there is at the conclusion of each story/illustration an analysis which identifies (1) injustice motivating the hero to act and (2) evidence that responses were guided by indiscourageable good will for all involved. Please reread this story in order to find commentary on the injustices and the good will responses.

WORKS CITED

Hanh, T. N. (2012, April 25). *Sojourners*. Retrieved April 25, 2012, from Verse and Voice: www.sojo.net

Holy Bible, The New Revised Standard Version. (1997). New York: Cambridge University Press.

Maguire, M. C. (2015, April 10). *Oxfam Ireland*. Retrieved April 10, 2015, from Oxfam Ireland: www.oxfamireland.org/heroes/meet-our-heroes

Soelle, D. (2001). The Silent Cry: Mysticism and Resistance. Minneapolis, MN, US: Augsburg Fortress.

CHAPTER 6

EXTREME HEROISM: INTEGRITY AND THE DAILY ACT OF BEING OURSELVES

Meddling with the Creator's Finest Creation

It was the late Thomas Merton, American Trappist Monk, who said "The beginning of love is the will to let those we love be perfectly themselves, the resolution not to twist them to fit our own image." (Merton, 2013) Extreme heroes are those who let others be perfectly themselves while looking for constructive ways of resisting those who work tirelessly to make others conform to their expectations. Maintaining one's own integrity, while encouraging integrity in others, is one of the most courageous things humans are tasked with doing and a never-ending challenge to maintaining extreme heroism.

A very helpful book pertaining to this subject, helpful in analyzing and understanding human diversity, is one by David Keirsey and Marilyn Bates entitled, "Please Understand Me". (Keirsey, 1984) Keirsey and Bates were both students of Carl Jung's personality theories. The title of their first chapter is "Different Drums and Different Drummers", is an apt metaphor for human diversity and in the same chapter they use the term "Personal Job Description". In a perfect world, everyone would be expected to hear and march freely to their own drum-beat and each would have a clear understanding of their own Personal Job Description.

But in an imperfect world, there are many who have yet to recognize their own drumbeats or have recognized them so powerfully that they feel compelled to have others march to the same beats, or die... figuratively or sometimes literally. Extremist groups typically take it upon themselves to try forcing the rest of the world to hear the beat they hear and then conform, or else. Their favorite targets are those still searching for themselves who are particularly susceptible to the certainty that comes with those having absolute knowledge.

While they consider themselves brave, courageous and even heroic in some sense, historically they have shown little appreciation of a world filled with infinite drum beats and infinite job descriptions and have no intention of honoring that reality. In reality they are found at a different place along the heroic spectrum. They occupy space where heroism has come to mean good will but only for a select few.

In a perfect world everyone acknowledges diversity and the obligation we have to live in concert with it. In a perfect world we would know, say, by the time we finish high school, what our personal options are for responding to injustice in our lives, however small of large. We would know about primitive responses: passive, do-nothing responses and aggressive, do-violence responses. We would know that neither of these is effective in restoring justice, even though both are used frequently by others.

We would also know about the many preferred responses to injustice – about the law – about how and when to use the law, and when to appeal to legal authorities. We would know about and have great respect for the power of certain words. We would in fact be extreme heroes by virtue of our expert use of words as effective responses to injustice such as the various ways of speaking prophetically.

We would know about and generally trust in the power of gentleness, kindness, good will, and mature love to guide us in choosing certain words and actions. We would have ideas about how best to use our individual gifts and talents in responding to injustice. We would know something about the principles of teaching and the use of stories and parables, along with what our options are in regard to responding as whistle-blowers.

But in the real world, we know very little about these options and are therefore likely to respond to injustice in primitive ways – every time. If we favor passive responses without being aware of our tendency to do so, we are quite likely to respond passively repeatedly. Or, if we favor violence without knowing that it is our inclination, we will most likely respond to injustice violently, again.

But in an imperfect world there are people still listening for a beat or looking for a perfect job description well into their retirement years. Some of them may die without realizing what they had to offer the world. Others may go about naively assuming that everyone else is a carbon copy of them and be terribly offended when others prove to be anything but a carbon copy.

In Keirsey and Bates' first book (Keirsey, 1984) they describe sixteen different personality types and within those sixteen types, infinite possibilities for many subtypes. Theirs is a helpful framework for understanding others partly because they make no attempt to define absolutely everyone's type or description. They simply provide the general framework and a few tools for analysis that take us to a certain point of understanding and then it's up to us to do our individual analysis.

In a perfect world society has something called team-work, but in an imperfect world there are fewer teams and more individuals standing alone as would-be dictators. Those who successfully and lovingly resist the expectations of dictators can be called "persons of integrity" or "extreme heroes" who take risks by working harder than others at being themselves while encouraging others to do the same thing.

Extreme Heroism Required From Jim and His Mom

One of Jim's earliest memories was his mother's eyes…icy blue, intense and boring-into-him as if asking: "Who do you think you are?" She could vary the question by putting emphasis on a different word like

"WHO do you think you ARE?" each time pressing harder for an answer and never averting her gaze. When Jim couldn't return her gaze, Mom demanded, "Jim LOOK at me!" and then she would start the questioning again.

Jim at age-8 honestly had no answers to her question. He had no idea what that question even meant, but he sensed an unspoken question which was "Who are you to argue with your mother?" and a worse question, "Who says she cares about your opinion?"

In a perfect world, were Jim not so young, and if he believed the questions were genuine he might have been able to say, "Whoever I am, I am different than you, Mom. I don't think the way you do, partly because I'm a child and partly because I'm different. I have opinions too and an obligation to express them to you with love and it would be nice if you would do the same." However, Mom's questions were not designed to solicit information…they were designed to silence, squelch, intimidate and humiliate.

Her questions were successful. By the time Jim entered high school he had learned the virtue of silence. Silence was the one place where he could exercise his integrity and therefore a tiny bit of extreme heroism. He maintained his real self in a place where conformers like Mom couldn't get at him.

"Hello Silence, my old friend, I've come to talk to you again…" (Simon, 1964) was the first line of a Simon & Garfunkel song being played on the local radio stations in the 1960s, over and over again which Jim listened to every day. This became his unspoken mantra. Silence is where he could be, most of every day, saying nothing or as little as possible, listening very carefully and thinking many things; having opinions but not sharing them.

He was a frustration to his teachers who had difficulty drawing him out of himself and into friendly dialogue, because Jim knew very little about that. Yes, Jim had found a way and a place where he could be an extreme hero. It would be a long, long time before he found a voice and the courage for sharing his thoughts with others in order to expand the reach of his extreme heroism.

In order that this book be usable as a teaching tool, there is at the conclusion of each story/illustration an analysis which identifies (1) injustice motivating the hero to act and (2) evidence that responses were guided by indiscourageable good will for all involved. For example: **(1) Injustice at home of course is common where children can be victimized by parents and where parents can become victims of their children's injustice. (2) Jim's response to injustice as he experienced it with his Mom would have to evolve through trial and error which is what a lot of children do. When all was said and done he loved his mother and respected her, so his response of retreat and silence was a good one considering his alternatives which are few for most children.**

Extreme Heroism…Jim and His Dad

Jim and his Dad, Big Jim, had a different relationship. Little Jim always knew that he liked his Dad but at the same time was afraid of him… fearful of being Daddy's little helper around the farm where they lived because that always got Big Jim super-frustrated when Little Jim who couldn't hammer a nail straight or saw a piece of lumber correctly or understand how plumbing or electrical wiring worked.

Big Jim assumed like a lot of young sensate fathers that his first-born son would be a "spitting image of himself"; that they would fix together, design together and engineer things together around the farm…forever and ever. It didn't go that way. One day Big Jim was so angry with little Jim that he threw up his hands in despair and barked some awful words which seared Little Jim's psyche…"You are as worthless as a *@%&!" he shouted.

The words would have made perfect sense to another adult, but they served only to cripple Little Jim. He and his Dad never worked together again after that day…not even on the simplest things. Fortunately their relationship did not end there.

For reasons unknown, Big Jim took another tack where his son was concerned. He was after all, a strategist as well as an engineer. He set his sights on teaching Little Jim, not fixing him, not redesigning him or re-engineering him; his "indwelling hero" emerged. Those were the days of the dawning of the automobile, the spread of public highways and the rise of roadside motels in the aftermath of the Great Depression. It was then that Big Jim started showing Little Jim the world they lived in.

There were frequent road trips for the family. Many were made to the new National Parks popping up around the country. The National Parks became classrooms where Big Jim taught his son about the earth, nature and wildlife.

Little Jim's respect and admiration for bear, moose, wolves and other big game grew with each trip; he learned quickly that taking pictures of wildlife were OK…killing them was not, unless you were hungry. Simultaneously there were lessons about the earth and mountains and the rivers which coursed through them, carving canyons and forming deltas. There were many trips across country to see the accomplishments of engineers…the railroads connecting the east coast to the west coast…. amazing bridges spanning deep canyons, rivers and gorges…new dams to capture and save vast quantities of fresh water…mammoth generators and turbines creating electricity for many cities and towns across the continent.

There were never any tests or examinations for Little Jim…only show and tell…and by this Big Jim continued to dazzle Little Jim with the things human beings could accomplish as a team. Big Jim become an extreme hero by giving up any idea he had of raising a son in his own image. He traded it for a menu of choices from which his son might one day choose for himself.

Among the many things he wanted little Jim to learn was how to survive another economic depression like the Great One should it ever happen again. By the time Little Jim was a teenager and the family had moved into the city, Big Jim had already awakened Little Jim on many a morning after a circus or carnival had left town. When these traveling entertainers had pulled up stakes, usually during the night, Jim and Jim would descend upon the dust of an abandoned midway.

Together they would stroll through the fair-grounds or parkland where the tents and booths had offered food, shelter and entertainment. These were places where people took money out of their pockets to play a game or pay admission only to drop some in the dust. Big Jim and Little Jim would start walking shoulder to shoulder as soon as there was morning light, watching for reflections off the face of dropped coins. Big silver and half-dollars were the easiest to spot...quarters, dimes, nickels and pennies were the hardest...but there were lots of them.

Big Jim walked and pointed ahead into the dust...soon Little Jim caught on and they were able to spread out until their pockets were filled with heavy coins. Behold a way to survive another day during a Depression!

On other days, usually Saturdays, Big Jim awakened Little Jim before the city street-washing trucks had scoured the downtown. There too it was 'heads and eyes down' as they walked along the sidewalks watching closely the base of parking meters where people took change from their pockets.

On other weekends Big Jim and Mom would awaken Little Jim early in order to walk the city dump looking for usable castoff furniture and other items. They found edible heads of lettuce and relatively fresh produce which stores and restaurants routinely dumped at the end of a day. No tests...just show and tell...things to keep mind.

In order that this book be usable as a teaching tool, there is at the conclusion of each story/illustration an analysis which identifies (1) injustice motivating the hero to act and (2) evidence that responses were guided by indiscourageable good will for all involved. For example: **(1) Through no fault of his own Jim was going to have quite a different personality from that of his Father, but their differences would seem like a great injustice to Big Jim for a while. (2) Big Jim's response was extremely heroic in that he chose to accept the abyss between he and his son and be resolved to building other kinds of bridges between them across which the two of them might cross one day and meet.**

Little Jim never became an architect or an engineer – that was not part of his drum beat or personal job description - but he did develop respect for people who design, build, fix and otherwise make life easier for others. He also developed sensitivity to feelings and familiarity with the variations in human feelings which eventually brought Little Jim to a career as a psychologist and a psychiatrist. By the time Big Jim died he and Little Jim had the tools for reaching across the chasm between them – sensate thinker on the one side, intuitive feeler on the other - quick decision maker versus patient perceiver. (Keirsey, 1984).

Parenting is as fertile a field for acts of extreme heroism as any battlefield, fire or medical emergency where the opportunities for extreme heroism never stop presenting themselves.

* * *

Jim's Mom was a hero too within the narrow frame of a woman's life on the Western Frontier and a woman living through the same Great Depression as Jim's father - a woman conceiving and giving birth at home without pre-natal care or continuing medical care - but her acts of heroism were imperceptible much of the time to Little Jim. It wasn't until he had reached the age of maturity and compassion that he awakened to the world around him which included his mother's own acts of extreme heroism which he could imagine even if he hadn't witnessed them. Henry Wadsworth Longfellow, a contemporary of Jim's mother, observed, "If we could read the secret history of our enemies, we should find in each [one's] life sorrow and suffering enough to disarm all hostility." (Longfellow, 2011)

A hundred years later Joan Chittister wrote, "Compassion for the other comes out of our ability to accept ourselves. Until we realize both our own weaknesses and our own privileges, we can never tolerate lack of status and depth of weakness in the other. " (Chittister, 2013) Nor will we be able to tolerate individual differences.

Our greatest challenge as extreme heroes often comes down to maintaining our integrity (Roberts, 2003) while facing powerful forces pressuring us to conform to standards which may or may not be appropriate for us. Even our most important institutions, religious and otherwise, can be guilty of imposing the wrong expectations on its members in order that they march to a particular drummer and cater to a particular job description. Episcopalian Clergywoman Barbara Brown

Taylor recognized this in her own life when she wrote, "I thought that being faithful was about becoming someone other than who I was, in other words, and it was not until this project failed that I began to wonder if my human-wholeness might be more useful to God than my exhausting goodness." (Taylor, 2009)

WORKS CITED

Chittister, J. (2013, July 25). *Sojourners.* Retrieved July 25, 2013, from Verse & Voice: www.sojo.net

Keirsey, D. &. (1984). *Please Understand Me: Character & Temperament Types.* Del Mar: Prometheus Book Company.

Longfellow, H. W. (2011, November 30). *Sojourners.* Retrieved November 30, 2011, from Verse & Voice: www.sojo.net

Merton, T. (2013, September 16). *Sojourners.* Retrieved September 16, 2013, from Verse & Voice: www.sojo.net

Roberts, G. D. (2003). *Shantaram Page 370.* New York: St. Martin's Griffin.

Simon, P. &. (1964). *Simon & Garfunkel Lyrics Archine.* Retrieved April 13, 2015, from Song Lyrics: www.sglyrics.myrrnid.com/index/htm.

Taylor, B. B. (2009, August 18). *Sojourners.* Retrieved August 18, 2009, from Verse & Voice: www.sojo.net

CHAPTER 7

HEROIC PROFILES: HOW WE OURSELVES RESPOND TO INJUSTICE

Becoming Self-Aware in Terms of Injustice and Extreme Heroism

In a perfect world, say by the time we finish high school, we would know what our personal options were for responding to injustice in our life, however great or small. For example, we would know about the two most primitive responses which are also the most typical: (1) passive do-nothing responses and (2) aggressive do-violence responses. We would know that neither response is the most effective in restoring justice even though they are frequently employed by many people.

We would also know about preferred responses to injustice: (1) the law; how and when to use the law; when to appeal to legal authorities, etc. (2) the word; knowing about and having great respect for the power of certain words as effective responses to injustice; we would know the best ways to speaking prophetically.

We would know about and generally trust in (3) the power of gentleness, kindness, compassion, good will plus mature love to guide us in choosing certain words and actions; (4) how best to use our individual gifts and talents in responding to injustice; (5) the principles of teaching and the use of stories and parables and (6) how and when to respond as whistle-blowers.

But in the real world we know very little about these options and therefore we are more likely to respond to injustice in primitive ways...every time. If we happen to favor passive responses, without knowing we tend to do that, we are more likely to respond over and over again by doing nothing. If we favor violence without knowing we are inclined that way we will most likely have violent responses, over and over again.

But if there has been evolution beyond primitive responses then we might already favor the involvement of the law and will more easily "call the cops" or otherwise appeal to authorities in settling disputes. If we have the money, we are more likely to call our lawyer and direct him or her to take legal action. However, if we're a musician writing and singing about life injustices, we'll be more likely to write another song about each new injustice...especially if it sells records and DVDs.

If we're a screen-play writer we'll prepare another script for exposing the injustice by way of a movie, television series or a Broadway play. If we're a poet we'll write another poem. If we're an artist we'll draw or paint another picture.

If we're an actor we'll take another role in a movie about injustices. If we're a dancer we'll choreograph another dance. If we pray, we'll pray about each injustice. If we know what's good for us to be guided by, in choosing our responses, we will be guided in everything by indiscourageable good will for victims and perpetrators.

Yes, in a perfect world we will know ourselves so well and our options for responding to injustice, we will always be more likely to exhibit extreme heroism and be willing to adapt or change as circumstances dictate. We would pray at the beginning, pray in the middle and pray at the end. We would consciously strive for balanced approaches as we respond. If it's an heroic inventory that's wanted then "this is what I am, this is what I do and this is how I am mostly like to reveal extreme heroism abiding in me".

Passivity – Not Responding to Injustice – An Ancient Favorite

It should come as no surprise to find there are two common ways of responding to injustice; both are aptly called old-fashioned because they've been around since the beginning of humankind: one is passive; the other is its opposite. One does nothing; the other does something violent. We'll talk more about violent responses later, but suffice it to say that repeated failures in achieving justice through these means have not deterred most of humankind from continually trying to restore justice by unjust means.

While we know that being a door-mat leaves us feeling terrible, we nevertheless keep going back to this ancient recourse unless there is a lot of pressure to do something else. And in case we think passivity is acceptable or justified by its frequent usage, it might be helpful to remember how the ancient Hebrews referred to passive responses as wicked. Wickedness or passivity was such a serious offense the Psalmist begins the first of 150 Psalms by denouncing wickedness. "Happy are those who do not follow the advice of the wicked." (Holy Bible, The New Revised Standard Version, 1997)

It was a young man in the 15th Century who happened to pass a Benedictine Monastery and who, out of desperation, knocked on the door, which led to his becoming the Abbot of the Monastery at age 21. He went on to become John Trimethius. His knock on the door was a first step on the way to becoming a champion of words…words as a response to every kind of injustice.

He would declare passivity as a completely *unacceptable* response to injustice and write: "We are going to render an account to God, not only for our idle words, but also for our ill-considered silence." (Trithemius, 1500) But remember, there is a big difference between well-considered silence and ill-considered silence. One could be at prayer and it only appear to be ill-considered silence. One could be planning some non-violent yet powerful response and it only look ill-considered in that moment. The silence of Little Jim in the previous story was well-considered, given his age, circumstances and the desire to survive.

Violence as Passivity's Evil Twin

Political Activist Mary T. McCarthy said of violence: "In violence we forget who we are." (McCarthy) It is not good to forget who we are because in forgetting who we are, we forget that we march to a rhythm especially suited to us and that we have a unique and special job description to fulfill (see Chapter 5). Often, after countless passive responses to injustice, we hear people say "something snapped", "I just lost it." and "I became the incredible hulk," which often means "I gave into violence."

Repeated failures in achieving justice through violence have not deterred humankind yet they continue trying to restore justice by "blowing things up". The ancient Hebrews had a special word for violence just as they did passivity…it was called "evil" because it carried with it a desire and an intention to inflict pain on those who hurt us first. Understandable, yes; but seldom helpful in the long run.

When Passivity Clashes With Violent Aggression

It had been a big day at school…a sunny day in May as Steven's senior year was rapidly drawing to a close. Graduation rehearsals, senior parties and plans for the prom were already in full swing in celebrating seventeen years of education. Steven had been a shy, passive 17-year-old striving to overcome his shyness by doing something courageous, therefore it was no coincidence that he gravitated to a Reserve Officer Training Program (ROTC) in his school. There was no question that the uniforms, the weapons training, learning to march and learning to give orders to others in small groups and larger groups, were all good for Steven; they increased his confidence and helped draw him out of his shyness.

By his senior year he had advanced to the highest levels of leadership that high school ROTC could offer. At the annual Military Ball he was acclaimed Second in Command of the school's regiment. He appeared to be on a path to a military career…university ROTC would be next and then a direct commission upon entering the Army, but all of that was about to come to an unforeseen end.

It was late in the afternoon and long shadows had already formed on the east side of the campus and over the majestic old building where Steven and a thousand others had just spent the day. Most everyone had gone home, but Steven stayed later than most to put away helmets and weapons in the school armory, following the day's activities and the Annual Drill Down, a competition among junior cadets that was watched by the entire student body in the school gymnasium. It was one of those 'last man standing' kinds of events and Steven that year was one of several senior officers conducting the exercise.

At the end of the Drill Down a single cadet was to be honored for surviving the ordeal of commands, standing, turning, marching, and handling weapons using World War II, vintage M-1 rifles. Winning this event himself a year earlier had been one of Steven's several accomplishments in ROTC. After the Drill Down, tired but gratified, Steven had climbed the stairs to the floor where his school locker was located.

He retrieved a few books for the evening home-work assignments and walked back down to the main floor and the exit. Still in uniform, he donned his military cap with its new oak-leaf insignia, pressed the release bar on the door and stepped outside. Out of the corner of his eye he saw two female students standing nearby, leaning against a car looking his way and talking, but from the other side he saw a blur as something hit him on the side of his head, almost knocking him down.

The blow knocked off his cap and scattered school books all up and down the steps and into the street. Looking around for who and what had hit him, a question had already leaped into his mind asking WHY, as if the answer might make him feel better! In a quick mental inventory which only took 2 seconds to conduct, Steven could think of no reason to justify what this person had just done.

He saw a tall rugged-looking boy, maybe a year or two older, poised to hit him again, someone who was a complete stranger to Steven. The only identifying marks were the dark blue coveralls he was wearing, like those worn by boys studying auto repair in the school annex. But Steven needed answers and the question must have been written all over his face because instead of hitting him again, the stranger let it be known that he was advocating for a friend who happened to be one of the junior cadets from that afternoon's competition. His friend had also been one of those disqualified by Steven near the very end of the Drill Down, meaning the friend might have won, if Steven hadn't disqualified him.

What the young man had seen from afar in his balcony seat was a tap on his friend's shoulder by Steven, signifying that he was out of the competition. What he could not see was his friend's slight false-move that had disqualified him, yet he saw none of this from his balcony seat and he believed he had witnessed an injustice. Through his violent response, trying to trump an apparent injustice with another, a military career was derailed because this wasn't Steven's first trauma...the blow to his head had opened an old emotional wound.

Steven's personal response to the injustice done to him however, was familiar and passive. It never occurred to him to fight…he wanted instead to understand. It never even occurred to him to seek legal recourse through an appeal to school authorities.

Steven didn't know about such things. He had never seen it happen to anyone in his family. It never occurred to him to tell his parents about the incident and it certainly never occurred to him to tell any of his friends.

Instead he would bear the burden of what is now called *bullying* for most of his life. For all practical purposes the story ended there without the emergence of extreme heroism. While passivity may have shielded Steven from more violence in that moment it did not protect him from the self-degradation and self-labeling as coward which followed him for many years.

While there was a perceived victim…the young man who "almost won the Drill Down" that day, and a perceived villain, Steven the Cadet Officer, there was also a perceived hero in shop coveralls to his two girlfriends. He would conclude and believe, perhaps for the rest of his life, that he had corrected an injustice done to his friend. In truth he had compounded the injustice.

Steven responded as he had learned to do, passively; the others responded as they had learned to do, violently. There was pain on both sides but no progress for anyone…and no gain.

> In order that this book be usable as a teaching tool, there is at the conclusion of each story/illustration an analysis which identifies (1) injustice motivating the hero to act and (2) evidence that responses were guided by indiscourageable good will for all involved. For example: **(1) Injustice in classroom settings continues unabated through high school and sometimes college and university. Sometimes, if we're lucky, it becomes apparent that one person's justice becomes another person's injustice. Relationships in high school can unravel very quickly if these conflicts occur frequently. (2) Steven's passive response to his tormentor was inappropriate but that's partly because he didn't know he had any options. He honestly believed there was nothing he could do except surrender his ambitions and dreams.**

Aggressive Violent Responses – Ancient Favorites

In the real world, in every culture, there are those who are very sensitive to injustice. They sense it, feel it, even smell it, yet that alone is not enough to bring out extreme heroism. It takes sensitivity to injustice combined with knowledge of the appropriate responses available to us guided by a trust in indiscourageable good will…to draw out such heroism.

Without this knowledge, without good will, many opportunities to live extremely heroic lives will be missed.

December 17, 2008, London, England - A British-Iraqi doctor, 20 years old, by the name of Bilal Abdulla was convicted of conspiracy to murder in setting off bombs in London. In talking to Associated Press reporter Robert Barr, he explained his motives…believing like many others before him that there was nothing he could do to reestablish justice besides doing injustice in return.

Bilal was outraged by the violence in Iraq following the overthrow of Saddam Hussein. He told Barr. "I wanted the public to taste what is going on, for them to have a taste of what the decisions of their democratically elected murderers did to my people. I wanted to challenge their government's proposal that war brings peace, that preemptive strikes will bring peace to this country." (Barr, 2008)

Seems logical and sounds very familiar...people have been rationalizing this response since humanity lived in caves...toward governments...toward masses of people...toward individuals. When we respond this way to governments and masses, it's called terrorism. When we respond this way toward individuals it's called bullying.

In order that this book be usable as a teaching tool, there is at the conclusion of each story/illustration an analysis which identifies (1) injustice motivating the hero to act and (2) evidence that responses were guided by indiscourageable good will for all involved. For example: **(1) Injustice done to one's family or country weigh heavily. Victims feel obliged to do something even if it's wrong. Perhaps driving them in many cases is a fear they will be branded cowards by others if they don't retaliate. Extreme heroism is not cowardice. It is the highest form of heroism. (2) Bilal's response...violence for violence...does not qualify as extremely heroic because it always, always makes things worse. The same can be said for the following:**

December 17, 2008, New Delhi, India – See how far back in time some men or some women will reach to justify a primitive response to an injustice: An Indian television news anchor got a call from a man who called himself, Imran Babar. Imran wanted to explain a bombing of a luxury hotel in Mumbai. It wasn't enough to have done the violence; he wanted to use the violence to teach and explain.

The blast killed 171 innocent men, women and children and injured 250. Imran's grievances started with (1) the 2002 riots six years earlier in Gujarat state where more than 1000 men, women and children, mostly Muslim, were killed; (2) next was the 1992 demolition of the ancient Babri mosque by Hindu mobs sixteen years earlier and (3) finally back to an injustice he perceived committed by the government of India over the disputed Himalayan region of Kashmir.

Reporter Emily Wax of the Washington Post said Indian officials suspected he was inspired by an even larger list of grievances stretching back to the 17th Century including the continent's partition in 1947 that created the independent nations of India and Pakistan. (Wax, 2008) In a culture of vengeance and retribution, where extreme heroism has been smothered by violence, the outcome is predictable. About this culture it was Dr. Tahir ul-Qadri, a London-based Pakistani politician and Islamic scholar of Sufiism who wrote, "They [terrorists] can't claim that their suicide bombings are martyrdom operations and that they become the heroes of the Muslim Umma [global brotherhood]. No, they become heroes of hellfire, and they are leading towards hellfire. There is no place for [such] martyrdom and their act is never, ever to be considered jihad." (ul-Qadri, 2010)

*April, 2013; Bombing of the Boston Marathon...*As nearly as anyone can tell, the bombing of the Boston Marathon in 2013 by Dzhokhar and Tamerlan Tsarnaev, was a response cut from the same cloth as all these others. Tamerlan's motives in particular were conceived in the injustice he perceived as the fault of the United States back in his homeland, the Chechen Republic of Russia. His response was so like so many others, each one thinking to himself/herself that injustice can be corrected by inflicting another injustice.

Think for a moment about the injustices born of racism known so long and so fully by Black Americans and other people of color in the United States. It was in this crucible of "cumulative injustice" that Martin Luther King, Jr. observed for himself and about which he wrote, "Our lives begin to end the day we become silent about things that matter." (King Jr.) Our lives also begin to end the day we feel trapped inside a human hamster cage shaped by endless cycles of injustice/passivity or violence with no other way out.

September 11, 1999, Fort Worth, Texas – 47-year-old Larry Gene Ashbrook burst into his church sanctuary and opened fire, killing six before killing himself. Authorities were *mystified* as to his motives. That was the front-page.

The back-page was some undetermined injustice committed against Larry which had apparently wounded Larry emotionally. He turned against those whom his father favored…his church community. While we don't know who or what hurt Larry, Associate Press writer Megan K. Stack reported, "We know that his father had died without leaving him anything, leaving everything instead to his church, Pleasant Ridge Church of Christ."

Should anyone ever ask you about your heroic profile you should be able to admit to passivity and violence as being something you are capable of, just to be honest, but then be quick to know if the law is also in your profile; if words are important to you and seen as powerful responses, and if so, what sort of words do you come by naturally? Perhaps prophetic words or teaching words? Talents? Special gifts? Whistle blowing? Know yourselves and be ready at all times to give an accounting of yourself and the kind of responder you are likely to be in the face of injustice.

Should we ever come to despair of our human reliance on passivity and violence, remember the words of St. Augustine who said of such things: "Hope has two beautiful daughters; their names are anger and courage. Anger at the way things are, and courage to see that they do not remain as they are." (Augustine, 400) As the late Charles F. Kemp, Professor Emeritus at Brite Divinity School said in a lecture: "Be angry, but don't DO angry." (Kemp, 1974)

WORKS CITED

Augustine. (400). *Sojourners*. Retrieved June 15, 2009, from Verse & Voice: www.sojo.net

Barr, R. (2008, December 17). Explosion conspirator says his goal was fear: Doctor convicted of conspiracy to murder says bombs had protest message. *Casper Star-Tribune*. Casper, Wyoming, U.S.A.

Holy Bible, The New Revised Standard Version. (1997). New York: Cambridge University Press.

Kemp, C. F. (1974). Professor Emeritus, Brite Divinity School, Ft. Worth, TX.

King Jr., M. L. (n.d.). *Sojourners*. Retrieved March 9, 2009, from Verse & Voice: www.sojo.net

McCarthy, M. (n.d.). *Sojourners*. Retrieved September 12, 2013, from Verse & Voice: www:sojo.net

Stack, M. K. (2009, September 15). *Fort Worth Star-Telegram*. Fort Worth, Texas, U.S.A.: Associated Press.

Trithemius. (1500). *Sojourners*. Retrieved July 30, 2008, from Verse & Voice: www.sojo.net

ul-Qadri, T. (2010, March 4). Retrieved April 15, 2015, from Al Jazeera: www.minhaj.org/english/oid/10354

Wax, E. (2008, December 17). *The Washington Post*. Casper, Wyoming, U.S.A.: Casper Star-Tribune.

SECTION II

EXTREME HEROISM: AN ARRAY OF APPROPRIATE RESPONSES TO INJUSTICE

CHAPTER 8

PRAYER AS RESPONSE TO INJUSTICE

As Long As We're Taking Risks Remember Prayer As Risky Too

On the whole our English-speaking world seems at best pessimistic about prayer and its influence in responding to injustice. At best it is vague about prayer and what exactly it means, but when nations turn to see what our more respected and articulate spiritual leaders have said or are saying about prayer they can't avoid being impressed by their conviction and their clarity in declaring that prayer can be "the real deal" and be hugely significant. Without a doubt there are many who are persuaded toward the efficacy of prayer and believe we all prove ourselves smarter when we take prayer seriously as a response for our own lives and in taking it seriously we realize that we can be engaged in a risky endeavor.

John E. Biersdorf, Dean of The Ecumenical Theological Seminary in Detroit, Michigan, implies such in his book "Healing of Purpose: A Spiritual Journey" that prayer is dangerous, meaning it can draw us toward action: "As an act of love, prayer is a courageous act. It is a risk we take." (Biersdorf, 1985)

At a time when the world was embroiled in a World War, Mohandas Gandhi in India was declaring: "Prayer is not an old woman's idle amusement. Properly understood and applied, it is the potent instrument of actions." Catholic Priest and Pastoral Minister, Henri J. M. Nouwen wrote in his book, "The Road to Daybreak" that "Praying is no easy matter. It demands a relationship in which you allow someone other than yourself to enter into the very center of your person, to see there what you would rather leave in darkness, and to touch there what you would rather leave untouched (Nouwen, 1990).

British Baptist Muriel Lester observed that "Prayer always thrusts one out into action sooner or later. One of its main functions is to induce one to think creatively; it stretches the imagination; it enables one to see things and people not as they are but as they might be." (Lester, 2010)

In a perfect world, say by the time we finish high school, we would understand prayer as a valuable option for responding to injustice; that simply entering a thoughtful, reflective relationship with some higher power is a valid first response in many situations of injustice for both children and adults. Some even argue that prayer ought to be the first option at the very top of our list of possible responses to injustice, that it should reoccur frequently throughout the process of responding to a particular injustice and be the last thing we do when justice seems to have been restored. Beginning prayers, continuing prayers and prayers of conclusion can all be formulaic prayers – prayers that follow a particular pattern like memorized prayers (i.e. The Lord's Prayer) (Holy Bible, The New Revised Standard Version, 1997) or they can be instinctive prayers that are natural, informal, off the cuff and conversational with the created reaching out to their Creator.

Prayer can be general appeals for relief or very specific requests for help but the important thing about prayer is the doing of it in order not to be passive in the face of injustice. As a response to injustice, even the most clumsy, awkward, rambling prayer is far better than doing nothing or doing violence. Prayers assume a power greater than our own seeking to partner with us. We never set out to right a wrong by our own authority alone...that would be foolishness; prayer in its doing is a recognition of personal limitations.

It is not the intention here to lay out a lengthy catalog of all the various forms of prayer. People have been praying and writing about prayer for a long, long time and there are many good books on the subject in libraries, bookstores and religious institutions, but here it can be said that prayer is a tool of the highest order for responding to injustice as an act of extreme heroism. Extreme heroes do not pray to a vindictive, punitive or petulant Creator, but to a restorative, gracious, and loving Creator. As Anne Lamott put it in her book "Traveling Mercies", that we can "safely assume that we've created God in our own image when it turns out that God hates all the same people we do." (Lamott, 1999)

Boy on the Big Yellow Bus

(This story is repeated from Chapter 5 for its example of childhood prayer.)

Billy was a shy farm boy who rode a big yellow bus to school every day - nineteen miles, one way, into the city – along a gravel country road from where he lived with his parents, down an asphalt-covered highway into town to Roosevelt Elementary. Roosevelt Elementary was a brand new school built on the south edge of town to accommodate rural children in the southern part of the county. Billy was nine years old, a student in the third grade.

Every other day was mathematics day, first hour after lunch, Monday, Wednesday and Friday…taught by "Miss Stone". Miss Stone was severe in her teaching methods and severe in appearance with her white hair tied tightly in a bun. She matched her intimidating look with an intimidating style of teaching which she believed was the best tool for prying open the minds of nine-year-olds.

From day-one of that school year, Billy lived in dread of mathematics class. To Miss Stone's credit, she may have been instrumental in Billy developing competency in two things: numbers AND prayer. In the evenings, as he thought about mathematics class the next day, he would pray to God for protection from Miss Stone.

On the mornings of math class he would pray on the bus as it moved down the highway on its way to the school. He prayed during every free moment of the early classes. Interestingly enough, no one had taught Billy to pray. His family was not accustomed to overt praying, so it has to be said that his prayers were instinctive.

Miss Stone's customary routine was to march the children to a long chalk board at the front of the room to solve math problems. She would walk up and down behind them slapping a long slender stick in her left hand with which she would suddenly and dramatically point to a math problem and ask questions of a trembling student and then hit them in the back of the head with her open palm if they couldn't fathom the correct answer. She was much like a certain Special Investigator on a current popular television show, NCIS, Washington. Yes, by today's teaching standards she would probably be dismissed for such a teaching style.

Billy seemed to get preferential treatment in that when HE failed to comprehend a problem, Miss Stone hit him so hard his head literally bounced off the chalk board! Billy's prayers changed from "protect me" to "help me understand and get the answer before she hits me!" Perhaps as an answer to his prayer, Billy began to perceive some of the answers; he began to learn.

More and more often and to his own surprise he would come up with the correct answer. The hits from behind became less frequent, but never stopped entirely. Still, it was a big improvement.

It would be a lie to say that Miss Stone was Billy's favorite teacher, but she was one of the most memorable. Perhaps Miss Stone really loved children and teaching, but her love, if that's what it was, was a hard thing for young Billy to detect. If Billy had already been a deeply traumatized child, Miss Stone might have pushed his trauma toward a psychotic break.

Billy never told his parents about Miss Stone. He never complained about her to them or any of the other students – it just didn't occur to him in those days when teachers ruled the classroom with impunity. It would appear on the surface of things that Billy responded passively to classroom injustice if we didn't know that he did in fact DID respond to the injustice...with constant, intense, unsophisticated prayer.

To his credit it never occurred to him to respond with violence. He never got sick in order to stay home from school. The only thing he did was pray for help from a higher power as nine-year olds understand higher power.

Prayer in the face of injustice qualifies as an initial heroic response and as on-going responses to injustice, even for adults. Sometimes it is the only immediate response available to those being victimized, and a far better response than doing nothing or responding violently.

In order that this book be usable as a teaching tool, there is at the conclusion of each story/illustration an analysis which identifies (1) injustice motivating the hero to act and (2) evidence that responses were guided by indiscourageable good will for all involved. For example: **(1) Injustice in classroom settings seems to have been common to both public and church-sponsored schools of the 1900s. (2) Billy's response if not out of good will per se was certainly respectful, and that is good will in itself. Respect, if it can be mustered, can be one of several appropriate responses toward abusive authority.**

It was a New York City bus driver, Stephen St. Bernard, who at age 52 responded to a 7-year-old girl falling from a 3rd floor window (St. Bernard, 2012) with a prayer much like Billy at age 9: "'Please let me catch her, please let me catch her', That's all I could say, 'Let me catch the little baby.'" At very least the prayer helped Stephen to stay focused; at very best he enlisted the help of higher power.

Before there was widespread concern in the world about climate change it was Cultural Anthropologist Margaret Mead who observed that "Prayer does not use up artificial energy; doesn't burn up any fossil fuel; doesn't pollute. Neither does song, neither does love, neither does dance." (Howard, 1984) Karl Barth, a Swiss Reformed Theologian pictured prayer in wartime as a most significant response to the enormity of every great injustice: "To clasp the hands in prayer is the beginning of an uprising against the disorder of the world." (Barth, 1945)

WORKS CITED

Barth, K. (1945). *Sojourners.* Retrieved July 30, 2010, from Verse & Voice: www.sojo.net

Biersdorf, J. E. (1985). *Healing of Purpose: God's Call to Discipleship.* Nashville: Abingdon Press.

Gandhi, M. (1945). *Sojourners.* Retrieved January 12, 2011, from Verse & Voice: www.sojo.net

Holy Bible, The New Revised Standard Version. (1997). New York: Cambridge University Press.

Howard, J. (1984). *Margaret Mead, A Life.* New York: Fawcett.

Lamott, A. (1999). *Sojourners.* Retrieved March 27, 2013, from Verse & Voice: www.sojo.net

Lester, M. (2010, September 2). Peace Quotes. California, U.S.: Fellowship of Reconciliation.

Nouwen, H. J. (1990). *The Road to Daybreak: A Spiritual Journey.* Colorado Springs: Image Books.

St. Bernard, S. (2012, July 17). (MSNBC, Interviewer)

The Greatest Of All Laws

"You shall love the LORD your God with all your heart, all your soul, and with all your mind, and with all your strength." Deuteronomy 6:4

"The second is this, You shall love your neighbor as yourself. There is no other commandment greater than these." - Mark 12:29-31

(Holy Bible, The New Revised Standard Version, 1997)

CHAPTER 9

RESPONDING TO INJUSTICE WITH THE LAW

In The Right Hands for the Right Reasons... The Law is Sweet

Moving beyond passive and violent responses to injustice, to better and better responses, has been a long and difficult evolution for humankind. Only slowly and painfully did nations crawl out of the primordial swamp and begun to walk upright through responses that would qualify as extremely heroic. Others at times seem to be lagging behind...plodding slowly toward more mature forms of law.

At different times and in separate stages most nations have turned away from "nothing' and "violence" to words-in-the-form-of-something which Judeo-Christians called The Law. The quotation above in this introduction is borrowed for this discussion because of its content which some argue, constitute the spirit of the law which was thought to have guided the development of their thinking over several centuries.

The Law was and still is a collection of words. These particular words are called rules and constitute promises for living together. The Hebrews gave credit for this transition and development within Judaism to the person Moses (Holy Bible, The New Revised Standard Version, 1997). The Law basically promised that if the people "did certain things" and "avoided other certain things" life would go well for them.

The spirit of The Law was that of indiscourageable good will for all people, therefore violations of indiscourageable good will were to be considered a violation of The Law. In practice The Law works well so long as we are interested in justice and fairness for everyone and do not use The Law to give an advantage to one member of the human family over other members of the human family. Unfortunately the strong are often quick to find ways to do just that.

Today we like to think of ourselves as a nation where everyone respects the use of law even though The Law continues to be subverted by the powerful to gain, keep and increase their advantage over the powerless, i.e. voter suppression laws in the 21st century; i.e. massive inputs of money by the rich to influence elections in favor of candidates who will promise to support the agenda of the rich. Other nations have had the same experience as ours in seeing the law as a necessary response to injustice but also as opportunity for some to gain unfairly.

In South Africa, a whole system of laws had become twisted in favor of the white minority over the black majority. In response to this the black majority eventually organized the African National Congress which fostered the rise of activist Nelson Mandela. Albert Lithuli, first President of the ANC, said to the Nobel Peace Prize Committee meeting in 1960 that "To remain neutral, in a situation where the laws of the land virtually criticized God for having created [people] of color, was the sort of thing I could not, as a Christian, tolerate." (Luthuli, 1961)

It should go without saying that The Law has not earned the complete trust of the people in any nation that it could have. The Law is far from perfect and the system everywhere cries out for people of integrity to examine the laws of their land wherever that land is and root out laws which give advantage to the already powerful. While enforcers of The Law often make The Law a license for doing violence to the defenseless, there are many times when The Law in the right hands as become a tool of extreme heroism.

Canada and the United States pride themselves on being nations of laws. The Law does help; it can stabilize; it's amazingly useful at times and far better than violence or passivity, but its usefulness depends on who you are and what you know about The Law. Just ask parents advocating for gun control laws that would keep military assault weapons off the public market; ask any rape victim; ask any victim of domestic violence crying out for justice; ask any child in a school where there are no programs in place to prevent bullying.

Law as Heroic Tool in the Hands of a Man Wearing a Skirt

Jon (Glionna, 2015) was an interesting, multitalented man...as diverse in his interests and abilities as any; admirable, brave and courageous...a hero by many standards. While he had been recognized for valor in Vietnam he was a staunch opponent of war as a response to injustice, arguing as many have that most war does more harm than good.

He was a science teacher at the local college. He donated hours and hours to community service where he lived and in communities far away in Central America and Africa. He was funny...amiable...and oh yes... Jon liked to wear women's clothing. He often appeared in public with his many friends; he wearing a skirt and a blouse; his friends wearing ragged jeans and flannel lumber-jack shirts.

For wearing women's clothing Jon had been mugged and beaten but he had become fearless in expressing himself because he had come to understand The Law and how to use it to protect himself and seek justice. Those who responded violently to him soon wished they had not; a little jail time maybe and a costly fine. His abusers learned to leave Jon alone and let him live his life as he saw fit.

Jon was an *extreme hero*...not just for military valor or resistance to war...not only for advocacy for the poor...but also as a champion on his own behalf and for others like him who shared the same values.

In order that this book be usable as a teaching tool, there is at the conclusion of each story/illustration an analysis which identifies (1) injustice motivating the hero to act and (2) evidence that responses were guided by indiscourageable good will for all involved. For example: **(1) The injustice being denied the right to choose one's clothing is one thing; the injustice of doing violence against another for their clothing choices is another. (2) Jon's response in using the Law to bring about justice for himself and his tormentors was extremely heroic. Restraining others from responding to things they don't understand with violence helps everyone. Exacting compensation for injustice done to us when no one else is willing seems very right to do.**

A Model of Extreme Heroism for Law and Victims

Suman and Manjit Virk immigrated to Canada from India and became residents of Vancouver, British Columbia, Canada. In 1997 their daughter Reena was murdered by a gang of Vancouver teenagers led by a teenage girl, Kelly Ellard, and a teenage boy, Warren Glowatski. (McKnight, 2010) We don't know if the Virks had a prayer life but we do know they responded to what happened by appearing faithfully for every hearing or trial during the years immediately following the wrongful death of their daughter. It seems probable that their faithfulness to the laws of their adopted country was fueled by some form of prayer life.

The laws of Canada and British Columbia were the only obvious tool they had for responding to the terrible injustice inflicted upon them – the death of a child in their adopted country which had promised them inclusion. Suman and Manjit became instruments of improving the justice system for British Columbia through a decade of grieving and listening – as many victims before them had done, while others did all the talking. Their story began in a time when the courts were focusing their considerable resources and power on offenders – not victims - a system called punitive justice which often serves to compound the harm already done to victims.

After thirteen years of their quiet suffering, someone in the B.C. legal system saw fit to give these long-suffering parents an opportunity to respond to their injustice in their own words - their own voices - actually sharing in conversations about the murder with others and with those involved. The avenue which opened for them is now called "restorative-justice-conferencing" *(RJC)*. RJC is just one segment of a comprehensive restorative justice program which focuses on victims AND on perpetrators, aimed at healing a multitude of broken relationships.

After careful preparation through conferencing, Suman and Manjit came to the point of meeting one of their two offenders, Warren Glowatski, face-to-face. "During the meeting they were able to communicate to Warren the effects of his actions...how he had impacted their lives." (McKnight, 2010) Ultimately Suman and Manjit came to accept what they believed to be Warren's heartfelt regret and his acceptance of some responsibility for what happened.

Together with the B.C. Justice System they concluded that Warren had suffered enough through incarceration for his part in Reena's death and that now he could pursue further correction living in the larger community. Everyone involved learned just how important words were...heroic tools...words of back-stories, confession, regret, remorse, fear, shared sorrow, shared pain, forgiveness...all words as valid tools for responding to the enormous injustice through extreme heroism. Warren was paroled in June, 2010, without objection from anyone in the Vancouver community or from Suman and Manjit.

At last report, Kelly Ellard, the other person indicted for Reena's murder, was still progressing toward a day when she might also participate with the Virks in the restorative justice program. Extreme heroism does not excuse nor ignore what Kelly and the others did, but it does thoroughly engage the perpetrators. It seeks a balanced justice... justice for the past and toward the future...for everyone possible in the whole community.

Imprisonment can be a tool of heroism, but not if it's separated from the indiscourageable good will of the community and a desire for restoration. Under the right circumstances prison can be the means by which many finally hear and acknowledge the truth about themselves thereby clearing the way for the emergence of more extreme heroism.

In order that this book be usable as a teaching tool, there is at the conclusion of each story/illustration an analysis which identifies (1) injustice motivating the hero to act and (2) evidence that responses were guided by indiscourageable good will for all involved. For example: **(1) There is Injustice in this story at many levels, the greatest being the taking of another's life…for being a newcomer, but there is yet another injustice for the victims of The Law itself, i.e. being left out of the conversation which in this case is made worse by language barriers and being a legal yet new immigrant to a country. (2) Suman and Manjit's initial response of patience and polite respect for the Laws of Canada served them well, but their most heroic response would come when they sat down to converse with one of the young men who murdered their daughter. Their extremely heroic behavior made them models of Restorative Justice in Canada.**

Extreme Heroes in a Crowded Court Room

Two mid-level executives named Frank and Carter were in their mid-40s when they met one summer morning across a crowded court room. It happened to be the day that Frank's lawsuit against a former employer was finally reaching the trial stage and jury selection was set to begin. It had been a long uphill battle for Frank getting this far; he was tired and frightened.

He had never sued anyone before…not even when he and his wife divorced a few years earlier. They had simply reached an agreement which gave each of them joint custody over their children and a reasonable monthly stipend of support. They called it a "good divorce"… possessions, house, investments, savings were not an issue. There was nothing material worth fighting over.

The divorce had been easy for everyone…even the court officials who finalized their agreement were impressed, but what Frank faced now was very different…lots of fear, grief, anger and resentment. Money issues were enormous…broken promises, loss of income and loss of professional reputation. He faced a former employer who had way more money than he could ever spend, so Frank had turned for the first time in his life to The Law to grant him justice.

Across the room, waiting his turn in the jury pool was Carter who was learning about Frank for the first time…standing up as it were through the help of The Law to injustice. As the judge explained the nature of the trial about to begin, Carter began to realize that he and Frank had walked the same difficult path only to become victims of the very wealth he so wanted for himself. As he listened to the grim tale of what had happened to Frank, Carter wished he had known the alternatives and possessed the courage himself to have gone to court years before.

As the jury selection began, each prospective juror was named and asked to stand and give reasons, if there were any, why they should not be chosen as jurors. Several jurors stood to cite personal work and family reasons and were excused. By the time Carter's name was called he knew he could not serve with good conscience…that his moment to help Frank was right then and there…in that very moment.

Painfully and hesitantly he told the judge and other jurors that he had himself had experienced wrongful dismissal and could relate so thoroughly to the plaintiff that he had already decided who was guilty and it wasn't Frank. "I know firsthand how some wealthy employers treat their employees. They think they own you and can get away with anything."

Glancing frequently at Frank's former employer who was also seated at the front of the court room, Carter went on to tell the judge. "If a lawsuit gets this far," he said, "there's probably something to it!" Frank turned in his chair to face Carter the whole time that he spoke. Their eyes met knowingly before Carter sat down.

A few moments later the judge told Carter he was excused.

As he walked out of the court room into the marble-floored hallway, he thought to himself, "What a strange sound…the heels of my shoes echoing in these hallways where so many others have come and gone, but no one from my family has ever been here before. I am the first." The newspapers reported two weeks later that Frank had won his case.

In order that this book be usable as a teaching tool, there is at the conclusion of each story/illustration an analysis which identifies (1) injustice motivating the hero to act and (2) evidence that responses were guided by indiscourageable good will for all involved. For example: **(1) Employer-Employee Injustice is like every other form of injustice in that it can be responded to passively, violently or, in this case, by way of The Law. Cases like these are often made more difficult by an imbalance of financial power before the Law can actually be imposed. (2) Taking an offender to trial is difficult but it can be a valid response to injustice provided it is done with objectivity and good will toward self and offender.**

The Law Tested By World War II

Perhaps one of the most dramatic demonstrations of the importance and right use of the law in history came at the end of World War II. "To the victors go the spoils" was rallying cry of some who wanted to exercise old fashioned violence for the injustice done by the Nazi government of Germany between 1936 and 1941. They wanted to put all Nazis in front of a firing squad and shoot them dead.

However there were those who argued for a more heroic response to these admittedly horrific war crimes. Leading the charge, a perfect advocate of The Law some said, was Associate Justice of the U.S. Supreme Court, Justice Robert H. Jackson, who would preside over the War Crimes Trial at Nuremburg. (Jackson, 1945) Jackson would have the difficult and laborious responsibility of hearing testimony from alleged perpetrators and witnesses, one at a time. Justice in Jackson's court would come one person at a time.

With Adolf Hitler having taken his own life, the most high profile perpetrator remaining was Hermann Goering, former aviator and German war hero of World War I, who many thought of, along with Hitler, as an arch villain of World War II. Because of Goering's military experience and recognized military heroism in a previous war, he enjoyed widespread popularity among the German people and even many Americans. There is every indication that Goering responded appropriately on occasion to the injustices of war, risking his life to save friends and defend the country during World War I, but in World War II Goering did not regard every citizen of his country as deserving.

When the Allied Forces from around the world rallied against Nazi forces and turned the tide of World War II, Reichsmarschall Goering voluntarily surrendered, believing that he would be recognized for his heroic defense of the nation in the past and be given a place in its post-war future. Justice Jackson however, stood in the middle between those who wanted a firing-squad for Goering and those who believed that Nazis like Goering should be given a role in shaping a new Germany. Among the latter were several of General Eisenhower's own staff members, high-ranking officers, who partied one night with Goering after his surrender only to be reprimanded a few days later by Eisenhower himself.

Taking a stand with Eisenhower, between these two sides, Justice Jackson became an extreme hero by risking his life, his stature as a U.S. Supreme Court Judge and the nation's credibility by insisting that justice be done for everyone through a proper trial of all the German military leaders. He championed revisions in international law which made it illegal for nations to ever do again, legally, what Germany had done...declare war on other nations without just provocation or to declare war on its own citizens. In 1946 Goering's deeds and ways of thinking, which included the systematic extermination of Jews, were put on display for the world to see.

In the end, Goering and scores of other military officers were tried and convicted of crimes against peace and humanity. (Lisciotto, 2007) Some were sentenced to death by hanging; some were given lesser prison sentences and eventually gained their freedom. Goering believed that what he had done by eliminating the Jews of Germany was consistent with his version of heroism done in defense of nation against a perceived threat. He had risked his life to save the lives of the elite while declaring Jews undeserving of any good will at all.

Goering, along with some others, was sentenced to death by hanging as a result of his conviction. On the morning of his scheduled execution he was found dead in his prison cell…like his Fuhrer he had turned to death…by suicide. Someone, not wanting to see him suffer further for his misjudgments, had provided him with a cyanide capsule, but not before Justice Jackson had succeeded in setting a new standard for the nations and international respect for international law.

In order that this book be usable as a teaching tool, there is at the conclusion of each story/illustration an analysis which identifies (1) injustice motivating the hero to act and (2) evidence that responses were guided by indiscourageable good will for all involved. For example: **(1) The injustice of War seems infinite. The results of it last for generations; (2) Our response to war is often more war…trumping one injustice with another injustice. Justice Jackson's trust in The Law with its penalties, as a better response to injustice by nations is perhaps a perfect example of the good that can come when the Law is in the right hands.**

There is a time for suffering when we have done wrong; a time for pulling down and taking apart, but there also comes a time for putting things back together again. Capital punishment interferes with that process. For heroism to emerge in everyone, the key to our prisons must never be thrown away, but always kept for a day when we are ready for them to be opened.

The law has limitations. Not all uses of law are heroic. The law can become a tool of ill-will just as surely as a tool of heroism. Nations have not made it illegal for the wealthy to use the law to their own advantage. Nations have yet to outlaw excessive wealth or poverty. Nations have yet to outlaw war.

In a perfect world everyone would know that perfect Law is to love the Creator with all their heart, all their mind, all their soul and with all their strength and their neighbor as themselves. (Matthew 22:27-40). (Holy Bible, The New Revised Standard Version, 1997) The real world has been struggling with this since the beginning of time. Before he died, Origen of Alexandria, one of the earliest Christians (192-254 BCE) wrote "The law becomes an 'old testament' only for those who wish to understand it carnally, but for those who understand it and apply it in the Spirit and in the gospel sense, the law is ever new and the two 'testaments' are a new testament for us, not because of their date in time but because of the newness of the meaning. For those who do not respect the covenant of love, even the gospels are 'old'" (Origen, 230)

WORKS CITED

Glionna, J. M. (2015, April 4). Retrieved April 17, 2015, from Los Angeles Times: www.latimes.com/nation/la-na-wyoming-cross-dresser-20150404-story.html

Holy Bible, The New Revised Standard Version. (1997). New York: Cambridge University Press.

Jackson, R. H. (1945). *Robert H. Jackson.* Retrieved April 16, 2015, from Robert H. Jackson: www.roberthjackson.org/the-man.nuremburgtrial/

Lisciotto, C. (2007). *Holocaust Education and Archive Research Team.* U.S.: www.holocaustresearchproject.org/trials/nuremburg/trial.html.

Luthuli. (1961). *Nobel Peace Prize Lecture.* Oslo: Nobel Peace Prize Committee.

McKnight, P. (2010, July 10). Help for the victims of crime - and the offenders. *Vancouver Sun.* Vancouver, B.C., Canada.

Origen. (230). *Sojourners.* Retrieved November 16, 2011, from Verse & Voice: www.sojo.net

CHAPTER 10

RESPONDING TO INJUSTICE WITH OTHER CAREFULLY CHOSEN WORDS

Prophetic Words Are Always Born Of Indiscourageable Good Will

So The Law took shape and slowly found acceptance among varieties of people around the world, yet in every instance it has eventually become clear that The Law was still not enough by itself. Further evolution was necessary toward other effective responses to injustice, and so it was that from written words of The Law there came the first spoken words known as prophecy.

Like The Law, Prophecy used words but the words would be arranged differently. They changed from "Thou Shall" and "Thou Shall Not" to "Here's The Thing That Will Happen if Things Remain The Same". These words, one could say would have "teeth" in them but not in a destructive way. The earliest stages of prophecy had "teeth" but not teeth for tearing; they were "teeth" for saving and rescuing, like a mother cat lifting and carrying her kittens to safety or a female dog doing the same for her pups.

While they were words born of good will, they often aroused fear because they spoke of doom or calamity. What the people had difficulty understanding, then as now, is that truly prophetic words are motivated by a deep concern and a fervent desire for restoring justice for everyone on either side of an injustice...the kind of love which families and friends sometimes have in performing an intervention for an addicted loved one.

While the prophetic impulse is still alive and well, it often gets led astray by ignorance of what constitutes a prophetic ingredient. Parents, spouses, friends, everyone really, often believe they are being prophetic when in fact they are persecuting their loved ones. Instead of helping, they give prophecy a bad name.

Some say that true prophetic responses have faded from all our private and public discourse, replaced unwittingly by words of ill will. There is a parallel here to failures among nations to develop a just world through the law. Just as The Law has been perverted to serve one but not the other, so prophecy through ignorance can metamorphose into persecution.

Words with these kinds of teeth are not meant to save; they are meant to devour. In his book, *Where Have All the Prophets Gone?*, Marvin A. McMickle, in effect raises the question (McMickle, 2006) "Where have all the people gone who can see what's going to happen if things stay the same, who COULD say something prophetic out of good will, but do not?" Part of the answer is that many have never learned to speak prophetically in the first place.

Prophetic speaking must be learned and the importance of good will in prophecy must be cherished. Good will makes all the difference in whether words become instruments of persecution or tools of restoring justice. Fortunately there are still examples of the prophetic voice alive and well today, such as that of American journalist Thomas Friedman (Friedman, 2008). His book "Hot, Flat and Crowded: Why We Need a Green Revolution and How it Can Renew" points prophetically to a planet becoming excessively hot, a climate increasingly unstable while populations are increasing at an exponential rate.

There's no hint in Friedman's writings of ill will toward anyone. He doesn't emphasize blame. Using sound scientific data with regard to climate change, he foresees rising sea levels displacing large segments of the earth's population inland, leaving fewer and fewer obstacles to keep us from trespassing each other's lives. In a spirit of good will for all, Friedman calls for a revolution in thinking and technological innovation in order to save the planet from burning up and the peoples from overcrowding.

One of the best definitions of prophecy I've heard came in story form from a lecture by the late Dr. John Stewart, former Professor Emeritus of Hebrew Scripture at Brite Divinity School, Texas Christian University, Fort Worth, Texas. (Stewart, 1974) This classroom illustration has all the elements of extreme-heroism-through- prophetic-discourse. It illustrates the risk, danger, power and good will being directed toward the listener(s) along with the threat of a dire outcome if certain things do not change.

It also shows the risk and danger for the prophet in speaking prophetically. It shows the target audience asleep and thus the need for powerful words to awaken them. It shows good will in deliberately selecting words and actions which make the story both prophetic and extremely heroic.

Extreme Heroism through Prophecy

As remembered from a Lecture by Rev. Dr. John Stewart
(Stewart, 1974)

A certain person…could be a man or woman…is walking through a residential neighborhood late one night after most people in the neighborhood had gone to bed. All the homes are dark except one where a strange flickering light can be seen through a large plate glass window in the living room.

The prophet's attention draws her to the flickering light until she realizes that (1) the flickering light is coming from a destructive fire and not from a fire-place, (2) that the family who lives in that home has gone to bed and is fast asleep, oblivious to the danger and (3) that if the fire is allowed to continue burning it will destroy the house and the family inside.

Injustice is written all over this situation so the prophet looks around searching for a heroic way to respond. She sees a brick lying in the gutter. She grabs it and with great effort heaves it through the plate glass window. The glass shatters and falls with a terrible crash! The prophet bellows at the top of her voice through the broken window, stretching each word as she urgently calls out - FIRE! FIRE! FIRE!

The parents asleep inside are startled...rudely awakened from deep sleep...and immediately angry at being awakened. They awaken their children and rush to the living room. At last they see the fire and realize something of what is going on.

They call the fire-department and soon a fire truck arrives to put out the flames. By early morning they have cleaned up some of the mess and called their insurance company. Repairs will be made eventually. New furniture will replace the damaged furniture. Floors and carpets will be replaced.

Justice will be restored. The family will be compensated for their loss. And just maybe, the family will find the prophet who saved their lives and offer her their heartfelt thanks. (Stewart, 1974)

In order that this book be usable as a teaching tool, there is at the conclusion of each story/illustration an analysis which identifies (1) injustice motivating the hero to act and (2) evidence that responses were guided by indiscourageable good will for all involved. For example: **(1) Injustice pending, as seen by first responders, is great responsibility to undertake. It is extreme heroism of a very high order. In this case the worst case injustice is loss of home and then loss of life. Passivity is not an option but highly crafted violence can be. (2) The strolling neighbor is forced by good will and limited resources to respond with violence...a brick through a window and loud verbal warnings. Damaged property is nothing compared to destroyed property which is nothing compared to loss of life, but such is the role of a prophet.**

* * *

The above is a portrait of the early prophets of Israel and is different from the ones many of us carry in the back of our minds...images formed when we were children...fearful, frightening, intimidating images of stereotypically angry old people yelling at other people. Those images are wrong but they remain in our heads until or unless they are replaced with true images of heroic prophecy.

In a perfect world true prophecy evokes a saving response along with gratitude, but in a real world the words are often not heard…perhaps not loud enough yet to awaken the sleeping. Meanwhile the avalanche of prophecy coming from the scientific community concerning global warming and climate change is not abating; if anything it's getting louder. The intended messages are being heard by more and more people and that is encouraging, but the sleepers are strong in their resistance, much to the despair of the heroic scientific prophets.

Most often, the reward for delivering this kind of prophecy is delayed… postponed. Ask any parent. Hardly a child living, at the time they first heard those prophetic words emanating from their parents, remembers embracing those words or perceiving the love that propelled them.

Fran the Prophet, Jill the Recipient of Prophecy

Fran and her three small children, Jocelyn, Judy and Jill, had spent the morning downtown at their favorite toy store. The store was a great and dazzling place for children and child-like adults to be, filled to the rafters with toys of all kinds…games, puzzles, books, gadgets, on and on. With much excitement they would gather at the cash register after a long shopping spree where Fran, Best Mother Ever, would pay for their purchases…a fantastic new toy for each of the girls.

Jill, the youngest, could scarcely contain her joy each time they shopped together and as the four of them stepped out the front door onto the street, she was always the first to erupt with happiness and joy, jumping up and down, giggling uncontrollably, so much so her sisters were moved to jump with her. They took turns hugging their mother proclaiming her The Best! Fran was pleased of course because it was so nice to feel the affirmation from her children and see their exuberance and appreciation. Sometimes it is fun being loved!

She herself was looking forward to the dessert and soft drink they would have at the shop across the street before starting home. To get there they had to cross a busy intersection with four lanes of traffic. Fran had her head down looking into her purse, double checking to be sure she still had her wallet after paying for the toys.

The girls were engaged in excited chatter as together they approached the corner and the traffic light. The girls knew there was a traffic light and they knew there was traffic to watch for but they were distracted by their happiness. Fran looked up just as Jill stepped off the curb without checking for traffic.

Fran screamed at the top of her voice…JILL STOPPPPP! It was a prophetic scream that would forever be etched in Jill's memory. Just as a bus went swooshing by, lifting their skirts in its breeze, Fran lunged forward to seize Jill's arm and forcibly pull her back.

She seized it with such strength it dislocated Jill's shoulder. They didn't know this right away, but they knew for sure that Jill was in pain. She broke into tears as much as from embarrassment as from the pain in her arm. Fran went from being Best Mom Ever to Worst Mom Ever, in Jill's young eyes.

Fran turned the girls around and hustled them back to the car in order to rush Jill to the emergency room at the hospital where it was confirmed that Jill's shoulder was dislocated. Jill was still in tears. Fran - Loving Prophet/Best Mom Ever - was filled with remorse. She was sorry for screaming…sorry for grabbing Jill's arm with such force… yearning for Jill's understanding and forgiveness which would not be forthcoming for many years.

In order that this book be usable as a teaching tool, there is at the conclusion of each story/illustration an analysis which identifies (1) injustice motivating the hero to act and (2) evidence that responses were guided by indiscourageable good will for all involved. For example: **(1) The threat of pending injustice is responded to by the only one who can see it coming…a parent crossing the street with her children. (2) The mother's response is prophetic at the price of minor violence which seems great to a suffering child. Provided the mother continues to respond with extreme heroism she will realize that the daughter could not have seen what her mother saw. Extreme heroism will be required for perhaps some time until the child has further matured.**

Parenting Is Very Fertile Ground for Prophecy

Parenting is literally full of prophetic opportunities because parents are responsible for teaching and raising the consciousness of their little ones…in other words, "waking them up". Prophetic opportunities become actual prophecy when we are guided in our actions by indiscourageable good will for our children, but as soon as we come at them with anything less, we can quickly become their persecutors. Parenting is not a license to persecute and without good will the loud voices and the rough handling are no more than noisy gongs. Prophecy as a tool of extreme heroism is almost never fun, but it is something all parents and good friends are called to do… "Friends don't let friends drive drunk."

Prophetic Style Evolves from Grave Danger to Profound Comfort

In a perfect world we reach a point where we realize that someone's suffering need not be prolonged. We continue to use prophetic words but now the words are rearranged to express "Done and Done", whether it's a child who has suffered enough, a parent who needs grace and understanding, a friend who needs mercy, a prisoner who merits parole, a death-row inmate needing clemency. In other words there comes a time when we are called to the next level of prophecy, which in a way is the opposite of the first except for the good will and better future.

The Hebrew prophet Isaiah, for example, is credited with auditioning that kind of prophecy. Prophecy Isaiah-style declares someone's suffering is enough and is coming to an end. Unlike the first type of prophecy, this prophecy foresees a bright, happy future even for those who once ignored a prophecy that could have preserved their lives as they were had they been willing to make some important changes.

This type of prophecy became apparent for Israel after its exile in Babylon for many years. By then they had learned to bloom where they had been planted and they had made Babylon a better place. For this they were freed to return to their homeland, to prosperity and happiness. Their exile had ended.

John had Suffered, John had Killed, John Had Matured Enough for Deliverance

By the time they met John, he was already starting his eleventh year of a life-sentence for premeditated murder. The place where they met John was the center of their very own church sanctuary. The time was late one warm summer afternoon in August.

Who were 'they'? They were members of a church learning to care for others in their large inner-city community. In the course of their studies they had become acquainted with many different kinds of people in many different, but common situations…the newly widowed contemplating life alone, again; the newly divorced contemplating a similar life; parents who had suffered the loss of a child; men and women who had suffered wrongful dismissal at the hands of unethical employers; a newly immigrated family suffering the agonizing loss of country; and many others.

On this particular day, they were meeting a man who had killed his wife and her lover. He had been in prison long enough by then to be called a prison trustee - someone prison officials considered not a flight risk. He came to the church accompanied by his prison chaplain and it didn't take John long to sense the emotional/spiritual maturity of this particular group of people.

Things like acceptance, openness, warmth, gentle eye contact were signs to John they could be trusted and that made it much easier for him to tell his story. He told of being convicted of premeditated murder - premeditated because he had suspected his wife of meeting another man and using their home as a place for a rendezvous. He decided to wait one day outside his home to see if the other man would come.

Parking his car down the street where he was far enough away not to be seen by his wife, yet not so far that he couldn't see a car approach his home and park. A man got out, whom he had seen before, sitting with his wife at a fast-food place. The man walked up the front walk to John's home, rang the doorbell and disappeared inside.

John sat with a loaded revolver for about thirty minutes before approaching the house himself. He let himself in a side door and tiptoed fearfully up the stairs to his bedroom. He opened the door to find, just as he suspected, his wife and the man having intercourse.

John raised his gun and fired, emptying the gun, killing the man and his own wife of 15 years. He walked downstairs, phoned the police and waited for them to arrive. He was expecting to be arrested, but he thought he could justify what he had done because he was acting within his rights as a husband.

John was tried for a ghastly response to an injustice…the usual 'trumping one injustice with another'. If he considered other responses he did not say, but he was sentenced to life in prison, with the possibility for parole, for the planning and the doing what he did.

For the gravity of the injustice imposed on him by his wife and her lover, the courts granted him the possibility of parole after ten years but now, here it was, thirteen years later on a Sunday afternoon…the day before his parole hearings began. It was one of those moments that people call the fullness of time…when the stars seemed align and to everyone it seemed that the time was right for this particular individual to move on to a good life…time for a blessing instead of a curse…time to begin a new life…time for prophecy, not with teeth, but with a feather like a dove.

John talked at length about his thirteen years in prison personally convinced of his innocence and therefore justified in pronouncing a death sentence for his wife and her lover. He described the change of mind and heart, soul and body over the years which gradually came over him…waves and waves of remorse. He had been forgiven over the course of his many years and was a recipient of so-called restorative justice which had slowly changed the way he thought.*

(*which some would call "repentance").

John went into prison an unfeeling person; self-assured, cocky; believing he could think no wrong nor do anything wrong. In prison he was awakened…his mind was opened to see influence he had on his wife's unfaithfulness. The church group listened and asked thoughtful questions realizing that John was teaching them valuable lessons about their own marriages and relationships.

After talking for over two hours they turned their attention to the table in the center of the sanctuary and to a service of Holy Communion. John had grown up in a church where communion was a part of worship so it felt like coming home. Together they prayed for John and his parole hearing proceedings...pledging their support should he ever need it from now until after his release. They said farewell to John and the chaplain who had accompanied him, agreeing with prison officials that John had suffered enough...that it was time for a new future.

In order that this book be usable as a teaching tool, there is at the conclusion of each story/illustration an analysis which identifies (1) injustice motivating the hero to act and (2) evidence that responses were guided by indiscourageable good will for all involved. For example: **(1) The injustice experienced by John must not be overlooked nor can the injustice experienced by his wife which led her to seek another man's affections. The greatest injustice is the taking of lives by John. (2) John's response to the injustice he experienced is not extremely heroic, but many are those who can understand John's behavior. In this case The Law demands restorative justice for John which may take the rest of his life, or not if he is paroled. In this case, a church community, acting as the voice and representative of the community, listen to John and the story of his restoration. They vouch for his healing and speak prophetically like the ancient prophet Isaiah who declared that a nation had suffered enough.**

* * *

Mahatma Gandhi prophesied Isaiah-style to the people of India that they had suffered long enough under British Rule; that their time of oppression was at an end; that it was time for relief from poverty and a time for prosperity and joy. Martin Luther King, Jr., prophesied Isaiah-style to African Americans that they too had suffered long enough from the effects of American slavery and racism; that it was time for them to take their rightful place in American society, sharing in the prosperity and joy. Nelson Mandela prophesied Isaiah-style from prison to the people of South Africa that their suffering under apartheid was coming to an end; that they had suffered long enough and it was time for joy. Oprah Winfrey, Helen Gurley Brown, Margaret Atwood, Mary Daly, Betty Friedan, Maya Angelou are listed among hundreds of women who prophesied to women and men, Isaiah-style.

The need for real prophecy – toothy and tender - continues unabated. Some need to hear prophecy of the first order while others urgently require prophecy of the second order. These days for example…a time for prophecy of the first order for the wealthy one percent of our population who control 99 percent of a nation's wealth – a heavy, weighty, deadly injustice and at the same time prophecy of the second order is needed for the 99 percent who are poor, saying "You have suffered long enough. It's time for you to share in the prosperity and joy."

We live in a time when scientists are offering prophecy of the first order to every nation concerning climate change and global warming… "If this and that do not change here's what you can expect for the future"…at the same time they offer prophesy of the second order to the planet…that the time has come for Earth's suffering to end. It's a time for serious prophecy to weapons makers and promoters of war and a time for hopeful prophecy to war refugees and war victims.

Many Christians maintain and support something called Divisions of Justice within their respective denominations. In checking the website of The United Church of Christ, a mainline denomination in the U.S, I found the following injustices listed on their Justice and Witness page… current issues deserving prophecy of the first order for some and the second order for others:

(1) Sentencing Disparities between Crack and Powder Cocaine, (2) Oil Gushing Uncontrolled into the Gulf of Mexico, (3) Troubling conditions at many work-places – low pay, few fringe benefits, harsh conditions, unfair treatment or just plain unemployment, (4) Fair Trade Futures Conference in Boston and a Holistic Approach to Business and Poverty Alleviation, (5) Standing Up Against Poverty, (6) International Day of Prayer for Peace, (7) Mental Illness Network and Disabilities Ministries, (8) Adult Sexuality, (9) Public Education, (10) Faithfully Healing (Healthy Eating and Living), (11) Workers Compensation

and the Terrorist Event of September 11, 2001, (12) Creating and Sustaining Green Congregations, (13) Clergy Burnout, (14) Stopping Mountaintop Removal – Coal Mining In The Appalachians and (15) The National Criminal Justice Commission Act of 2010. (Ministries, 2010). I am sure that the list has changed greatly since 2010 – some things added, some things still there and other things removed - but I am also sure that the list is being maintained wherever prophecy is greatly needed.

Imagine all the other lists of a similar nature on the websites of many organizations, including churches and one quickly gets a sense of the commitment among millions toward those issues still causing pain to our populations. Institutions like these strive for the day when justice will dominate the world and injustice will be minimal but today they must prophecy so the prosperity and joyful future can come.

The challenge for all of us, especially when we are sensitive to injustice, is not to be overwhelmed by multiple needs. We must learn to set priorities. We need to realize that none of us can be expected to respond to every injustice, but at other times the injustice with our name on it is the one which appears on our life's doorstep…right at our front gate.

However injustice comes to our attention we must be selective in responding. As Bishop Kenneth Untener wrote in 1979, a prayer for his colleagues in the Roman Catholic Church, "It helps, now and then, to step back and take a long view. The Kingdom is not only beyond our efforts, it is even beyond our vision. We accomplish in our lifetime only a tiny fraction of the magnificent enterprise that is God's work. We may never see the end results, but that is the difference between the master builder and the worker. We are workers, not master builders; ministers, not messiahs. We are prophets of a future that is not our own." (Untener, 1979)

British author Karen Armstrong, former Catholic Nun, in an interview with "The Believer" said, "There are times when you have to speak out against injustice and cruelty. But if you speak—and this is what Ghandi said—in order to punish or wound you will do more harm than good. The Dalai Lama said that to condemn injustice with hatred in your voice will make the injustice worse. A lot of fundamentalist spirituality is rooted in fear, and when they attack, they become more extreme. So it does no good to attack viciously. The thing to do is not rise to the bait." (Armstrong, 2012)

Prophetic responses are words...verbal formulations and arrangements of words which foretell the future...unhappy or happy. They are vitally important heroic responses to the injustice we encounter in the world. All of us need to have these options in our spiritual quivers so that we know they are there, that we are not without options, that we can turn to them at any moment and speak them...or write them.

WORKS CITED

Armstrong, K. (2012). (T. Believer, Interviewer)

Friedman, T. L. (2008). Hot, Flat and Crowded. New York, New York, U.S.: Farrar, Straus, Giroux.

McMickle, M. A. (2006). Where Have All The Prophets Gone? Cleveland, OH, U.S.: Pilgrim Press.

Ministries, U. J. (2010, August 11). Newsletter. Cleveland, OH, U.S.: United Church of Christ Website ucctakeaction@ucc.org.

Stewart, J. (1974). Lecture Brite Divinity School. *Brite Divinity School.* Ft. Worth: Lecture.

Untener, K. (1979). *Sojourners.* Retrieved October 15, 2013, from Verse & Voice: www.sojo.net

> "Even if I knew that tomorrow the world would go to pieces, I would still plant my apple tree."
>
> (Luther, 1530) **Martin Luther**

CHAPTER 11

RESPONDING TO INJUSTICE PARABOLICALLY: THE HEROIC ART OF PLANTING WORDS, IDEAS, STORY, PARABLE, METAPHOR, ALLEGORY

The Art of Planting Words

Much has been written of Roman Catholic Priest, Martin Luther... about his influence on the Protestant Reformation...but few of us realize that like other effective religious reformers in history, he relied on the extreme heroic practice of planting or incepting words through story, parable, metaphor, allegory and many other word forms. Historians love to quote Luther's famous apple tree story without stopping to ponder its appeal: "Even if I knew that tomorrow the world would go to pieces, I would still plant my apple tree." As we look closely at this poignant statement we see Luther's theology of words-as-seeds shining through and a concept known as inception.

As human response to injustice using words continued to evolve, there emerged more and more options for responding. Various cultures were able to move beyond law and prophecy to more sophisticated responses. They settled on the farmer-gardener-sower-seed image as they came to see words as a unique kind of seed…seeds that could be planted in the human mind and psyche.

Once planted these words, healthy ideas, healthy thoughts and truth were as capable as any plant of producing abundant spiritual food, spiritual fruit, spiritual shelter and spiritual shade. While they were at it they discovered reasons for why some seeds never realized their potential, borrowing from weather phenomena to explain the things that happened…the heat of criticism, the storms of controversy, the weight of human trauma…yet confidence in planting and inception remained high because even small, occasional successes more than made up for their many failures. In spite of the obstacles to seeds taking root, some DID begin to grow, sprout, mature and bear fruit abundantly and that brought about healing, restoration and letting in the light of understanding.

Extreme heroism assumes that life-producing words are more easily accepted and taken seriously when they come to the listeners from within…not from outside. Heroism at this level becomes teaching at its best because the teacher avoids the temptation to simply tell what he or she perceives as the truth and give the answers, knowing that neither, in all likelihood, will take root or last for long. Extreme heroes acknowledge and accept that while there are many obstacles to word-seeds taking root, growing, bearing fruit, they plant anyway…even if tomorrow the world they have known comes to pieces.

Conception and Inception

As we will see in a subsequent chapter, movies are a special class of verbal and visual word arrangements well suited as tools of extreme heroism. One such movie, *Inception* - starring Leonardo DeCapprio (Nolan, 2010), was a metaphor itself about the art of planting seeds in the minds of others. Although the story is told in Hollywood style it serves well to illustrate the objectives and intentions of all parables, stories, poems and other word arrangements.

Inception the movie, is about a team of people attempting to implant the seeds of good ideas and healthy thoughts into the subconscious mind of a potentially powerful and influential person while that person is asleep and dreaming. In actual practice this is already a highly sophisticated art form in the field of commercial advertising...planting certain ideas in the mind of an unaware public in order to persuade people to buy certain products. In designing these particular thought-seeds, television marketers have 30 to 60 seconds to plant the seeds and then they wait to see what happens to sales.

The concept of planting/inception, while thriving in advertising, has not found as much favor in religious circles perhaps because so many clergy are not as patient as they need to be about planting healthy ideas. Some prefer to tell...give answers and admonish. Eventually though, whether religious, advertisers, teachers or leaders, people have to ask themselves if inception/planting seeds as a response to injustice is worth the effort and is it really effective? Ask those advertisers who spend millions of dollars every year to buy 30-second sound-bites for the Super Bowl.

Can good thoughts, healthy ideas, gentle, kind and true words be more powerful than simply speaking the same truth directly? Remember Paul Archambault who heard himself described as a hero...how he immediately pushed back. The truth that we really are extreme heroes doesn't sink in just because someone said we were heroes. It probably helps to see the claim printed in a newspaper or see the medal that someone drapes around your neck, but even that may not be enough.

It ought to help when others testify to the reality caused by a hero they happen to know. It ought to help when people in authority declare we are heroes, but sometimes none of those things are enough unless there's a 'seed' poised to take root and grow up from within. Our job is to keep trying...continue planting, watering, nurturing or as some people like to call it...reconciling...reconciling the world to better ways of doing things.

The words "*You are deeply, deeply loved by God*", whether issued publicly or privately, can encounter the same emotional and spiritual push-back. Even Christians have difficulty accepting and humbly believing they might be priestly, saintly, holy, disciples or apostles… that they are greatly cherished, extremely valued and deeply loved by their Creator. As Mark Twain once lamented, "I could never tell a lie that anybody would doubt, nor a truth that anybody would believe." (Twain, 2015) Twain became a champion of inception through his books and stories.

More often than not, each of us will be forced as extreme heroes to go beyond direct methods of responding to injustice; it's that or risk being defeated in spite of our best intentions. Those who keep score of such things tell us that Jesus himself encountered resistance and so he responds to injustice by way of parable, sixteen percent of the time in Mark's gospel; in Matthew twenty-six percent of the time; in Luke thirty-two percent of the time. Much of the resistance he encountered was among his disciples. (Holy Bible, The New Revised Standard Version, 1997)

In interpreting parables for ourselves we should always assume there was something Jesus couldn't say directly to his disciples or to his audience, so we always take time when interpreting to ask: what it was that Jesus might have believed that he could not say directly. We look for clues within each parable…stories from some aspect of their common life together that revealed important and for some reason, unspeakable truths about another aspect of their common life.

Consider the love…the good will…the thoughtfulness it takes to conceive of a parable and then tell that parable or write a poem and share it or remember an apropos story and tell it, etc. It requires trust in others and faith in their innate ability to nurture a seed planted and bear its fruit unknowingly, sometimes long after the planter/inceptor has gone on to other things. It can be a challenging emotional task to think about something for that long, that lovingly and that carefully, about another person but just ask any survivor of alcoholism whether or not it's worth doing.

About the parabolic method and task, theologian Nicola Slee has written that at the heart of the parabolic method there "lies a recognition of the power of language in our lives, to awaken the imagination, to stir the will, to shape our very understanding of reality and to call us into being and response." She goes on to assert that the parabolic method "reconciles the secular, humdrum, everyday world of realism with the unexpected, the extraordinary, the realm of the transcendent and the divine." (Loades, 1990)

The Parable of the Unjust Judge, Luke 18:1-8.

"Then Jesus told them a parable about their need to pray always and not to lose heart...A judge that has no fear nor respect for anyone, not even God." (Holy Bible, The New Revised Standard Version, 1997) Perhaps Jesus was saying to his disciples indirectly that in their pursuit of justice they will encounter people who are fearless; people who have risen to positions of power because others respect this fearless quality. Perhaps Jesus was trying to say indirectly that it was futile to try to frighten a fearless person...old-fashioned prophecy simply won't awaken them.

Know that they can't even be frightened by the prospect of failure or the possibility they are wrong. Pray instead to God for guidance, day and night, that you might find other ways to plant the seeds of truth in that person's spiritual garden.

When a Community Wants to Understand What Went Wrong

Organizations, institutions, groups, families, churches, synagogues, mosques and many others, after repeated failures to get along with each other, often turn to specialists - professional interventionists – to help them understand what happened, what went wrong and what they might do differently in the future. Whether it's an energy corporation concerned about their public appearance before an environmentally sensitive public or a nation's entire military force (Army, Navy, Air Force, Marines) concerned with a high incidence of rape and sexual harassment within their ranks or a business organization's staff mindful of their need for team work or a family where addiction issues are being avoided, or any other group…most all of us want to understand our dysfunction and learn how to change things for the better.

The following stories and lesson-plan for discovering 'what went wrong' comes from a Christian context and a fictional church/congregation. Those who stick with it from beginning to end should find it useful whether they are Christian, Jewish, Muslim, Hindu, Buddhist or Atheist because it illustrates what all groups of people must consider doing if they want to avoid future dysfunctional behavior.

Conclaves of Heroes, Communes of Faith, Real Friends, Real Family: All Thrive With Extreme Heroism and Perish Without It

All Saints Anglican Church in Somerville had been torn apart and seemed helpless to do anything about it so they turned through proper church channels to their superintendent and then their Bishop for help. Fortunately there was a system in place for handling these kinds of issues so the Bishop, after consultation with other Bishops, turned to The Reverend Meredith Chalmers, a specialist in these kinds of things and she was appointed to help the folks at All Saints. She telephoned the congregation's contact person and made an appointment to meet; a meeting to be followed by another meeting with three leaders of the congregation on a Wednesday afternoon in Somerville.

Ninety days later when the intervention was finished Meredith was able to write in her final report, that things that had happened to the congregation for which there were no protocols. The ways with which the congregation normally conducted its affairs had stopped working. Issues for which no one had planned, had mysteriously intruded upon and completely disrupted their normal communal life.

After many conversations, a set of questions were drawn up for the congregation to study and ask itself. What were the larger issues for the congregation and what were the larger issues for the Rector? What should they have done that they didn't do? What did they do that they shouldn't have? A weekend retreat for the entire congregation was planned with a program designed to help each member answer those questions.

Somerville in its early days had been a mining and logging town tucked away in the mountains of eastern Ontario, located at the head of a beautiful lake near the mines and log-harvesting sites. Ore and logs were exported to the world via the lake, 150 miles south to where an east-west railroad intersected with the long sinuous lake. On that site the logs were turned into lumber and the ore was refined as silver, gold, lead, mercury and other elements before shipping to southern ports.

That was their history; the mines were now closed and the logging companies had long since moved on to other parts of the world. The economy in Somerville had turned toward a thriving university, tourism, and retirement-aged people yearning for the mountains and the sight of abundant fresh water...and to a thriving yet illegal market for growing marijuana.

The current Rector, Chester Finch, had been in Somerville for over 35 years and had already been eligible for retirement for several years. He had been popular in the beginning, both locally and throughout the Synod. He had served on three influential Synodical committees and his older colleagues respected him greatly, but now he was growing older and living alone...his wife Lorraine had died 12 years earlier.

Chester's behavior with members in private became problematic. While the things he said privately to them would have seemed perfectly normal between an individual and their psychologist or between clergy, there were things that should not have been shared with parishoners. In one instance Chester had shared a dream with one parishoner so filled with dark and frightening images that it terrified the parishoner who turned in panic to another member for advice. Afraid that the Rector might be losing his mind the parishioner was desperate for appropriate responses.

It gradually came to light that the Rector was sharing similar things with other members in private that were sometimes meaningless yet always upsetting. Members didn't know how to respond, except eventually to share their experiences with each other. Everyone knew or thought they knew something was wrong but didn't have a name for it.

They withdrew emotionally from Chester and from church life which increased his loneliness.

Membership in the church prior to this had been divided between employees of the university on the one hand and working-class members of the community on the other. These latter were people who had been living in the community for two or three generations before the newcomers started coming. Newcomers for the most part were well educated, affluent and from other parts of the nation and the world; the latter were less well-educated members whose parents had migrated from eastern Europe in the 1950s.

Those who had known Chester for a long time loved him deeply because he had encouraged them when some were new to Canada and struggling to climb out of poverty. Their loyalty to him was fierce because he had helped them and that had brought stability to the community that earned him and the congregation great respect from non-church members. Chester also related well to the university employees, professors and technicians alike because he himself was well educated and able to understand the challenges of facing and teaching a young university crowd who came and went with every new semester.

He was good at welcoming and including newcomers and that produced a community with Chester at the center doing most of the relationship maintenance between the two major factions. When things finally took a turn for the worse it was manifest in three ways: (1) membership decline, (2) church income decline, and (3) members in conflict with each other over what to do about Chester's behavior. The affluent members wanted to appeal to the Bishop to force Chester's retirement; the poorer members wanted no such thing because Chester had taken care of them in their time of need and now it was time, from their point of view, to take care of Chester.

The more practical-minded university-based members prevailed. They were accustomed to systems that planned ahead like all good citizens are supposed to do and take care of retirement needs long before that time comes, so they did an end-run around the others and appealed secretly to the Bishop. The Bishop used his authority to have Chester take a 3-month leave-of-absence during which Meredith, the specialist, was summoned. She rented a room for 90 days and spent part of that time getting acquainted with key members.

In time she would introduce members of the congregation to the parabolic method of extreme heroism. After days and nights of interviewing and listening to people Meredith called for a congregational retreat for a Friday night, all day Saturday and Sunday afternoon, promising clarity and a better future for everyone about all that had gone wrong, what was happening to them and what they needed to do differently moving into the future. The weekend meetings ended on Sunday afternoon with a summons to reconvene 30 days later with the Bishop present for sharing their findings, thoughts and insights about the past, the present and about the future.

Everyone agreed to meet and spend the weekend together but Meredith didn't tell the congregation that she was going to use something called a parabolic response to the injustices they had been suffering right up to that night. On Friday of the retreat when everyone had gathered in the church basement for a potluck dinner and after they had eaten, Meredith began proceedings by saying, "You have been through a lot of pain and suffering in the several months and years. It's important that you learn from what has happened so that new things can happen from here on out."

"However we're not going to re-live all the things that went wrong. That would be too painful to go through again, so we are going to approach this by talking about other things. This might seem peculiar to you at first but actually it isn't peculiar at all. Jesus responded to difficult issues by talking about them indirectly and that's what we are going to do and as we do, we will put ourselves in a position to hear God…not me nor anyone else…just God speaking to us about the things that have happened and where we ought to go from here."

"You will recognize this as a method which Jesus used frequently according to Mark, Matthew, Luke and John. When there were things he didn't think he could speak of directly, he spoke of it indirectly by telling a story. For the next several hours together we're going to hear several of the parables he told; we'll speculate on what it was that he couldn't say directly to strangers and his disciples in order to see how they might apply to us."

"There seem to be a lot of issues for us to deal with and there are, but we will be talking about these things indirectly...not directly. It will be up to each of us to be aware of God 'speaking' to us from within through an inner voice and higher power. If everyone is clear about what we're going to do or clear enough…we can begin."

"There will be two breaks tonight during which you might decide to withdraw from the weekend. Simply tell me and the group your decision before you withdraw. That's all that's asked of you. Tomorrow there will be four such breaks."

"In the 30 days which follow before meeting with the Bishop, you will be asked to keep a journal in which you record the thoughts and insights which come to you tonight and every night thereafter. In the future you will be able to refer to your journal in your conversations with the Bishop. You should start using your journal now. I will be present with you at the meeting with the Bishop in order to guide you through the extraction process."

Needless to say, everyone went on a high emotional alert. Initially there was some disappointment that they weren't going to revisit all the hurts and some had a hard time seeing how they could "talk about one thing by talking about another thing" but they were willing to try. Not surprisingly they had never been asked to do this kind of thing before.

What follows next is the lesson plan used for that weekend:

INTRODUCTION TO AN EXTENDED CONGREGATIONAL MEETING

- Trying times have come to All Saints Anglican Church
- We do not want the events of the past to reoccur.
- This weekend event will deal with the traumas we have suffered but *only indirectly* using the parabolic method…in the sense of a parable:
- What we do and say this weekend will include the parable to which we compare the events, facilitate reconciliation between members in order to substitute behaviors that will result in a better future.

(Show Cartoon from Christian Century Magazine, February 12, 2008. Life in the church is evolving.)

OVERVIEW OF SESSION ONE & TOMORROW'S FIVE SESSIONS

- **In Session 1** - Greetings and welcome.
- Goal of these sessions – to understand what went wrong, to identify the changes we can make that will set us free for a worthy purpose as a united people.
- Our Methods: Biblical and Parabolic
- Talking about one thing
- In order to talk about another thing (the traumas)
- Rule #1 for the next 10 hours is to NOT talk about the injustices of our past
- Rule #2 keep those injustices in the BACK of your minds as we progress..
- Rule #3 Start noticing the connections between our experiences of the past with the experience of others, some many generations removed, and others more nearly our contemporaries. This is to make it easier to communicate effectively with each other in the days to come without being re-traumatized.

- **In Session 2** we will begin with INJUSTICE and how the biblical people, historically, have responded to it. We will look at their...

o Primitive responses to injustice – **doing nothing**

o Primitive responses through **various forms of violence**

o A mother's Christmas letter in praise of child's sensitivity.

o Charles Manson's motives and response to injustice

- We will introduce a preliminary sketch of how the biblical people evolved from passivity and violence into legal and prophetic ways into the ways of Jesus.

o The coming of The Law and Legal responses (Holy Bible, The New Revised Standard Version, 1997)

o The coming of Prophecy and continued evolution

- **In Session 3** we will explore extensively the coming of Jesus and the parabolic response to injustice

o A meditation on Psalm 1.

- o Was Jesus direct or indirect?
- o How parables are constructed.
- o Were parables used often or sparingly?

- **In Session 4** we will take time to study and share our own histories of responding to injustice...how we were taught...and how far we've evolved since.
- o Primitive response A...doing nothing because we taught to do nothing
- o Primitive response B....premeditated retaliation, revenge, payback
- o Legal response...I reported the incident to higher authorities, or not.
- o Prophetic A response...I went public with my opinion...writing, speaking.
- o Prophetic B response...I went public again...encouraging and affirming.
- o The Way of Jesus...I responded in ways that left open the possibility of reconciliation.
- o How would you analyze your own response patterns? (Find one person with whom you are willing to share your self analysis. Get their feedback.)
- o Conclude with a reflection on the prophet Isaiah, his father (Amoz), his uncle the King (Amaziah) (Holy Bible, The New Revised Standard Version, 1997)
- **In Session 5** we will conclude by dwelling on Jesus-type responses in injustice and explore as honestly as possible the implications for us for the future. We will look at the future of church by exploring case studies of injustice using contemporary examples clipped from the headlines.
- Please notice the time line for our five sessions located on page 7. See you in the morning at 9:30 for a continental breakfast. We'll begin Session Two at 10AM sharp.

BREAK – CONCLUDE SESSION ONE

BEGIN – SESSION TWO

- **In Session 2** we will begin with INJUSTICE and how the biblical people, historically, have responded to it.
- o Primitive responses to injustice – **doing nothing**

Bible Study of Psalm One – The Great Problem of Doing Nothing

This is the first of 150 Psalms (Holy Bible, The New Revised Standard Version, 1997) which is remarkable when we consider what other themes the Psalmist might have chosen for a beginning. Perhaps the Psalmist considered wickedness/passivity/doing nothing to be the first and greatest obstacle to a meaningful life. Notice the use of all caps which is biblical code for God or Yahweh as indiscourageable love.

"Happy are those who do not follow the advice of the wicked, or take the path that sinners tread, or sit in the seat of scoffers; But their delight is in the law of the LORD and on his law they meditate day and night. They are like trees planted by streams of water, which yield their fruit in its season, and leaves do not wither, in all that they do, they prosper. (Holy Bible, The New Revised Standard Version, 1997) (Notice that reference here to 'the law' is not just any law, but *the law of the LORD* which is indiscourageable good will.)

The wicked are not so, but are like chaff that the wind drives away. Therefore the wicked will not stand in the judgment, no sinners in the congregation of the righteous; For the LORD watches over the way of the righteous, but the way of the wicked will perish." (Holy Bible, The New Revised Standard Version, 1997)

- o Primitive responses through **various forms of violence**
- • Remember Charles Manson and his legendary responses to the injustices he perceived in the world. It might seem a stretch now to talk about Charles Manson and the ways he responded to injustice, but remember the injustices he perceived all the way back to 1971. One of the reasons he gave for killing several people in California was punishment for humanity's neglect of the environment, the animals and the melting of the polar ice-caps.
- ▪ Here we are almost 40 years later and humanity is still talking about these very things. His anger with humanity for an infinite number of wrongs led him to say in his last interview that if he could he would kill everyone on earth for the wrongs they had committed. (Discuss)
- ▪ Copy of a mother's Christmas letter in praise of her child's sensitivity.

- In a recent Christmas letter to family and friends a young mother spoke proudly of the year's achievements by her children and added the following about her youngest: "He has the memory of an elephant! If we forget one little family rule or get something wrong, he always calls us on it!" (Discussion)
- Are we all born with a natural sense of injustice and unfairness? If so, what happens to that sensitivity? (Discussion)
- ▪ "Injustice anywhere is a threat to justice everywhere." - Rev. Dr. Martin Luther King, Jr; Letter from Birmingham Jail. (King, 1963)

BREAK – CONCLUDE SESSION TWO

BEGIN – SESSION THREE

- **In Session 3** we will explore extensively the coming of Jesus' parabolic response to injustice
- Matthew 13:34-35 "Jesus told the crowds all these things in parables; without a parable he told them nothing. This was to fulfill what had been spoken through the prophet: "I will open my mouth to speak in parables; I will proclaim what has been hidden from the foundation of the world." (Reflect on the usage of parables. Talk about the love that it takes to not do nothing, yet respond to injustice parabolically. (Holy Bible, The New Revised Standard Version, 1997)

o A meditation on Matthew 3:13-17. "Then Jesus came from Galilee to John at the Jordan, to be baptized by him."

o John the Baptist was the last in a long line of faithful people who had tried to do the right thing in the face of the injustices they had encountered. Until Jesus there had only been a handful of individuals who tried responding with unwavering love, good will and compassion. David was one, but most were inconsistent about their love…sometimes petulant, violent and vindictive.

o Jesus did not condemn any of them. His baptism by John seems to say, "You and those who preceded you were never completely wrong even in responding badly…at least you responded. Now I show you a better way. Let's take the law and prophecy to a whole new level to the level of indiscourageable good will, compassion and forgiveness for the whole world. (Discussion)

- o "No abyss of evil can hide from [Jesus] through whom the world is reconciled with God. But the abyss of God's love encompasses even the most abysmal godlessness of the world." (Bonhoeffer, 1941)-Dietrich Bonhoeffer (From *Meditations on the Cross*)

BREAK – CONCLUDE SESSION THREE

BEGIN – SESSION FOUR

- **In Session 4** we will take time to study and share our own histories of responding to injustice...how we were taught...and how far we've evolved since.
  - o Primitive response A...doing nothing because were taught to do nothing
  - o Primitive response B....premeditated retaliation, revenge, payback
  - o Legal response...I reported the incident to higher authorities, or not.
  - o Prophetic A response...I went public with my opinion...writing, speaking.
  - o Prophetic B response...I went public again...encouraging and affirming.
  - o The Way of Jesus...I responded in ways that left open the possibility of reconciliation.
  - o How would you analyze your own response patterns? (Find one person with whom you are will to share your self-analysis. Get their feedback.)
  - o Conclude with a reflection on the prophet Isaiah, his father (Amoz), his uncle the King (Amaziah) (Holy Bible, The New Revised Standard Version, 1997)

BREAK – CONCLUDE SESSION FOUR

BEGIN – SESSION FIVE

- **In Session 5** we will conclude by dwelling on Jesus-type responses in injustice and explore as honestly as possible the implications for us for the future. We will look at the future of church by exploring case studies of injustice using contemporary examples clipped from the headlines.
- **Case Study:** "A high school senior was beaten up after school by a classmate who thought the senior had victimized a third party, the classmate's friend. Beating up the one whom he perceived as the perpetrator was his response...a classic example of evil attempting to trump another evil."

- "The senior's response at being beaten, much like a rape victim, was to do nothing, at least for a while. Going to the school principal or teachers did not occur to him. Turning to his friends or parents did not have much promise either, but after a time the loneliness from being the only one who knew what happened was too much for him. He turned to his father.
- "His father quoted scripture: Romans 8, "All things work together for good for those who love God" (Holy Bible, The New Revised Standard Version, 1997) which the senior wasn't equipped to understand. His father seemed to be advocating 'doing nothing'…just take it…so he did."
- (Discussion. If this were your son what would you say to him? What would you advise him to do? What options would you see open to him?)
- Read Luke 9:28-36a. Speak of this as a turning point in which The Law and the Prophets were put to rest. "This my Son, my Chosen; listen to him" (Holy Bible, The New Revised Standard Version, 1997)

CONCLUSION

Read Luke 7:18-20, 22, 28. John the Baptist asks about Jesus. Is he "the one who is to come or are we to wait for another?" Jesus directs John's disciples to go and tell what they have seen and heard about the blind, the lame, the lepers, the deaf, the dead and the poor." (Holy Bible, The New Revised Standard Version, 1997)

Is it ever too late to learn new ways of doing things? Can those who have always been passive learn to be bold? Can those who've always solved things through violence, learn to solve them through good will? Can those who've always solved things through legal recourse…turning to higher authorities… learn to solve problems through the Spiritual law of indiscourageable good will? Can those who have always solved things through confrontation learn to solve things gently and kindly and even indirectly using parables as Jesus did?

Questions for individual reflection between now and our meeting with the Bishop

- What place have passive responses had in our congregation?
- What place aggressive responses?

- What place The Law? Was it used heroically or to gain the advantage?
- What place Prophecy? Was it used heroically or to persecute?
- What place Prophecy B? Was affirmation, reassurance offered or withheld.
- What place The Way of Jesus?
- What place our artistic, creative gifts?

Meditation on Psalm 8; God as Essence of Indiscourageable Good Will (Holy Bible, The New Revised Standard Version, 1997)

It isn't wrong to resist injustice. Even when we resist badly, we're not completely wrong in standing up against something that isn't completely right. It is better than not resisting at all.

Teach one another by example that it is good to resist injustice, even the small inequities, because those moments prepare us to resist the larger inequities like racism, corporate wrong, governmental wrong, institutional wrong, parental wrong-doing, etc.

Reward one another with recognition and appreciation for seeking and doing high-level responses to resist wrong and unfairness.

Look not only for heroes among our nation's military, but look for them also in our communities, churches, schools, businesses and wherever people are actively seeking justice, fairness, equity, balance, harmony and peace in this world.

PRAYER FOR THE MOUNTAIN TOP

The stories, parables, metaphors, allegories, poems, figures of speech chosen for the weekend were chosen for their potential to help participants see that while they experienced many injustices through their relationship with the Rector in recent years…partly due to his age and partly due to his religious authority they themselves had responded by doing nothing unless they wanted to count gossip. They would need to see how these responses were passive and therefore unacceptable… the worst possible response that they could have chosen…that this is what the ancient people called wicked. No one seemed to know how to be honest without hurting Chester or seeming to persecute him, so they did nothing, except further isolate him.

A second thing the stories and parables were designed to reveal indirectly was attitudes which had created tension between the university crowd in new-town and the uneducated poor in old-town. They were going to have to acknowledge this tension, the reasons for it and find ways to talk about it with each other before they could clarify their purpose for being the church in that town.

A third target was exposure of faulty thinking by Chester concerning retirement…how he had chosen to live without a pension so that the congregation could afford to keep him…not realizing that he was creating dependency and tipping the balance of power. He and they had been naïve about the church's viability if they couldn't support a pastor financially…that Chester was probably wrong for thinking that congregation would bail him out when he reached retirement age by selling church assets in order to support him. Hopefully they would see themselves as unrealistic in much of their thinking toward ministers as being immune to poverty and able to live in retirement without income.

A fourth thing the stories and parable were chosen to expose was both a blind trust in the hierarchy of the church and/or their hostility toward hierarchy. Some were inclined to look to the larger church to solve all their problems while others were inclined to solve everything themselves. In fact, as the evening of the retreat began the distrustful people exposed their distrust in the Bishop and his appointee, Meredith by staying home. They were conspicuous by their absence while the others were remarkable for their presence.

When Meredith's time with Somerville was over it could be said that they had had a remarkable experience with a new level of extreme heroism. They were amazed at the ease with which connections and insights popped into their heads… aha-experiences were plentiful to both rich and poor. They realized they were going to need some help in learning how to respond to injustice at heroic levels.

After reflection, those who attended the meeting were able to acknowledge their responses to congregational injustices were mostly primitive. Their favorite response was avoidance. They avoided and missed opportunity after opportunity and with each missed opportunity the situation got worse.

It was an American civil rights activist and founder of the Niagara NAACP, W.E.B. Du Bois, who spoke of seeds while admonishing African-Americans in New York to act now, not later, when he said "Now is the accepted time, not tomorrow, not some more convenient season. It is today that our best work can be done and not some future day or future year. It is today that we fit ourselves for the greater usefulness of tomorrow. Today is the seed time, now are the hours of work, and tomorrow comes the harvest and the playtime." (Du Bois, 1960) From this original inception came the national NAACP.

Their second-most favorite response in Somerville had been hurtful, mean-spirited words which were mistaken for prophetic pronouncements. Some favored legal responses but only if those responses promised to give them advantage. In the long run they admitted they had not taken the time to respond creatively or with good will.

Near the end of the whole process when meeting with the Bishop and Meredith, members shared excerpts from their personal journals and were able to freely admit that they had many opportunities to respond to several injustices but that they were so accustomed to doing nothing followed by brief sorties of persecution that they could be described as a primitive-parish in terms of their responses to injustice. They confessed to devoting almost no time to pray and to giving very little thought as to how they might employ good will in choosing their responses. Their third-fallback- position was The Law in terms of Church tradition and organization which they admitted to using for their own advantage.

Finally they admitted they had learned something radically new about the religious word repentance...that it meant changing the way they thought. For this they were going to need interim leadership to help them move in a new direction...that full-time leadership might be a couple of years away because they had so much to learn...so many bad habits to change. Thirty days later that interim leadership was realized with a female Rector, appointed by the Bishop to serve two years. Two years and thirty days later, a full-time Rector was called...to a parish who had found their voice, their courage and a way out of the old – primitive - ways of responding to injustice.

In order that this book be usable as a teaching tool, there is at the conclusion of each story/illustration an analysis which identifies (1) injustice motivating the hero to act and (2) evidence that responses were guided by indiscourageable good will for all involved. For example: **(1) Injustice in church, synagogue, mosque and all religious communities and non-religious communities have passivity and violent words as their most common forms of injustice. (2) Extreme heroism like that described in this example comes about only as communities of faith sincerely seek to understand what they did and did not do that got them into trouble in the first place.**

WORKS CITED

Bonhoeffer, D. (1941). *Sojourners*. Retrieved May 6, 2008, from Verse & Voice: www.sojo.net

Du Bois, W. (1960). *Sojourners*. Retrieved May 18, 2012, from Verse & Voice: www.sojo.net

Holy Bible, The New Revised Standard Version. (1997). New York: Cambridge University Press.

King, J. M. (1963). *Sojourners Magazine*. Retrieved April 2013, from Sojourners: www.sojo.magazine.net

Loades, A. (1990). *Feminist Theology: A Reader*. Louisville: Westerminster/John Knox Press.

Luther, M. (1530). *Sojourners*. Retrieved October 31, 2014, from Verse & Voice: www.sojo.net

Nolan, C. (2010). Inception. Hollywood, CA, U.S.: Warner Bros. Pictures.

Twain, M. (2015, April 22). *Desk Calendar*.

CHAPTER 12

RESPONDING TO INJUSTICE THRU INDIVIDUAL GIFTEDNESS

When Words Fail and All We Have Are the Pictures

When Angela Y. Davis spoke of Progressive Art as a tool for education, helping society perceive things it might not otherwise perceive, she also spoke of "the objective forces" affecting society and our "interior lives". In perceiving these objective forces as they impinge upon us from outside and from within, some are able to translate their perceptions into art forms and as soon as that happens they have already begun their response to injustice. Angela called this translation, "social emancipation". Whenever these kinds of responses are guided by indiscourageable good will, Progressive Art becomes an effective tool of extreme heroism.

So as society has learned better and more efficient ways of responding to injustice and has continued evolving along the pathway of words, it inevitably comes to the place where words meet their origins and at last they are born. Experiences of injustice...many of them extremely painful...produce mental images in the lives of victims, sometimes long BEFORE any words form. While the images wait for translation into words, prior to being spoken or imposed on paper, film or the internet, the victims must function as a kind of greenhouse that preserves the experience until the moment comes when words, still in the fetal stage, are finally thrust out of their womb and into life.

To speak of Progressive Art and other forms of giftedness, is to speak of that womb and its threshold, a place of conception and growth which precedes all word-responses (law, prophecy, story, parable, etc.) which eventually bring us to fruits of personal giftedness. Personal giftedness is about the unique talents and abilities that spring up from within, conceived in suffering and nurtured in the greenhouses of our memory. Behold, the twisting, swirling, shifting world of Progressive Art.

To illustrate this, start by remembering an experience of painful injustice, either for ourselves or someone else. In remembering the injustice we remember the pain and in remembering the pain, remember the images of that experience and in remembering the images, if we haven't done so already, remember the first words that emerged. In moments when the mist and fog begin to clear...when images are the clearest, they can be captured on canvas or told in a stand-up comedy routine or portrayed in a movie or sculpted into stone or molded into clay or sung as a song, depending on our personal giftedness. Not everyone can do all of these things, but everyone can do some of these things if they look for it and wait for it...wait for it...wait for it.

In every individual there is a pool of such gifts whether he or she is aware of it or not. It is called our artistic side - from there the individual, if they are patient, can choose a response to an injustice. Responses to injustice can take the shape of a painted picture or a photo captured on camera or a symphony or a song that sells a million albums, or a movie that exposes an injustice or a book that does the same thing but does in a way that it doesn't amount to slander or persecution.

In the more mountainous injustices like slavery, responses had to be simple and to the perpetrators seem manageable (as opposed to immanent threats). One such response to the misery of slavery was the act of quilting...piecing together various pieces of fabric hung on clothes lines in ways that carried messages. During times of slavery in the U.S. enslaved women were known to weave clues as to location of the so-called 'underground railroad' by which runaway slaves could make their way north to safe communities. Quilts contained directions for fugitive slaves who knew what to look for regarding safe houses and escape routes.

There is of course an inexhaustible supply of similar heroic responses preserved in the art of every generation. In 1994 the United Church Press in Cleveland, Ohio, chose an ambitious path toward publishing a 3-volume set of Progressive Art called "Imaging the WORD" (Lawrence, 1994) It was a companion to the Christian Lectionary*. Students of sacred literature could then study each art form for their "hidden messages"...a message that the artist believed they could not speak directly or openly, much like that of a good story or a good parable.

> (*The Christian Lectionary is a 3-year plan for a comprehensive study of the Bible.)

The following are stories of gifted responses to injustice which preceded the words which would eventually be born.

Extreme Parental Heroism – Giving What One Has of the Sacred

Steven lived in a time before education systems were only vaguely aware of a form of human behavior which we in North America now recognize as bullying. In those times, not that long ago, educators considered themselves helpless to do much about the injustice of bullying, so they did nothing. It was a wicked time in which our hero Steven had been beaten, humiliated and bullied, off and on, for years, on the way to and from school. Not knowing there was anything he could do about it he endured it by clothing himself in a cone of silence.

He was 17 years old before he broke that silence and he chose to break it with his father who was an odd choice because his father had always insisted that Steven solve his own problems. "Figure it out!" he would demand. But now Steven was desperate because he couldn't figure it out. He was having so much trouble focusing that it all came gushing out one Saturday morning while he was riding in the car with his father as the latter ran errands around town.

They had just come out of a new department store that fascinated Steven's father and put him in a good mood. Steven seized this feel-good moment and before his father could start the car, he dumped the whole story of his life of perpetual bullying. When he finished, all out of breath, there was a long silence and finally he asked his father, "What should I do?"

His father sat silently for what seemed like forever...so long that Steven was getting scared all over again. In retrospect Steven would later be grateful that his father didn't recommend boxing lessons or scold him for not being tough enough and thankfully, didn't offer him a lecture on manning up. What he DID say was kind of stunning considering what he knew about his father which didn't include anything like religious giftedness. His father never attended church and when he spoke of church it was not with fondness.

In fact his father was hostile toward religion for certain unknown injustices he himself had experienced in the church of his childhood. Along with this, Steven's father had come to associate and equate all of his own parent's flaws and inconsistencies, with the church, but in spite of all these things his father finally relaxed and visibly settled comfortably into his seat. He sighed and slowly said, "All things work together for good for those who love God."

Steven was underwhelmed. He had no idea what to do with those words. He would silently repeat them to himself, over and over, for many years hoping they would yield some hidden message. After all, it was what his father offered, so it couldn't be nothing...it HAD to be something. Decades later he deciphered the message after discovering that his father had quoted scripture, Romans 8:28, written by a man named Paul who was writing to Christians about responding to injustice. (Holy Bible, The New Revised Standard Version, 1997)

While the lasting significance of the answer escaped him for the moment, the immediate effect of the words was oddly calming... "for those who love God." In his own way Steven allowed as how he DID love God and so he guessed he could wait for all things to work together for good. His depression was temporarily displaced perhaps by thinking about what it means to love God.

Steven never mentioned the incident to his father again, but we can safely say that a seed was planted that day that may have been the only gift his father deemed worthy and fitting to give. He had looked into his personal gift-bag as it were and saw there a few religion-based-word-relics that, in spite of everything, seemed valuable. Obviously "All things work together for good for those who love God" had become meaningful to his father…so in effect he passed them along for replanting in the mind of a new generation facing new forms of injustice and old-fashioned bullying.

In order that this book be usable as a teaching tool, there is at the conclusion of each story/illustration an analysis which identifies (1) injustice motivating the hero to act and (2) evidence that responses were guided by indiscourageable good will for all involved. For example: **(1) Injustice often emerges even as we are seeking the help of others in addressing an injustice. At times like this it appears that very few people know much about helping others respond so they advise others to do the old tired and untrue passivity or violent aggression in some form. Only the wise try to do better. (2) Steven was fortunate to have asked someone who would respond with something wise.**

Extreme Heroism thru Writing Lyrics, Songs, Taping, Singing on YouTube

Some say that Dave Carroll of Halifax, Nova Scotia, is both a Canadian and American folk-hero…meaning he has been nominated and elected unofficially by the people of two countries using an increasingly common street-method on the internet and social media. Dave was a natural at being an extreme hero through his special giftedness which included writing lyrics and combining them with music he heard in his own head. The story of the public's response by the millions to Dave's injustice, is typical of a phenomenon others have experienced in using the so-called social media when responding to the injustices of their own lives.

Dave composed, sang, played guitar and made videos. Chances are good he did not think of his gifts as tools of extreme heroism but we can confidently claim they were. According to Brad Wheeler (Wheeler, 2009) writing for the Toronto *Globe and Mail*, Dave was traveling on a well-known airline as a professional musician – his guitar stowed in cargo with other luggage. This had never posed a problem before but this time when he arrived at his destination he discovered that baggage handlers had broken his $3500 guitar.

Picture Dave's initial response as an emotional one...very, very painful. His first visible response to this injustice was words in a formal report to an airline agent and then a showing to them of what had happened to his guitar. The agent thoughtlessly quoted official airline policy to Dave and denied any responsibility for the airline, leaving poor Dave standing in the wreckage of his livelihood with no immediate recourse. The injustice weighed heavy as he remembered the agent's shrug and his words 'nothing can be done'.

By the time Dave got back to Nova Scotia things were already erupting emotionally out of his recent experience and one them was a melody that later translated into words that would become lyrics. Using an old back-up guitar he started experimenting with words and melody that would soon strike similar inner chords with millions of others. Armed with his newly created song, Dave created a video of himself performing "United Breaks Guitars".

After posting it on YouTube, it was viewed overnight by five and a half million people. Viewings of the video spread like a virus because Dave's experience was so much like that of a lot of others that they responded to this injustice as if it were their own. While they apparently had not advocated for themselves, they were now set free to advocate for Dave by writing internet letters to United Airlines.

Their internet reactions reached United Airline and it wasn't long before the airline realized they had a public relations problem...not just with Dave Carroll but with millions of other travelers. They wisely responded by replacing Dave's shattered guitar and issuing a formal apology. However, the story did not end there.

Soon after, with Dave flying again as a professional musician on the same airline, taking off from Regina, Saskatchewan, landing at Denver

International Airport, again neither luggage nor new guitar showed up in baggage claim. This time the airline insisted Dave wait in baggage claim until his belongings arrived. By the end of the day that had not happened.

Dave could wait no longer and went on to Colorado Springs, Colorado, where he was scheduled to speak and entertain.* That night, Dave's audience in Colorado Springs happened to be a group of customer service executives for a number of large companies that include United and others.

> (*His belongings arrived three days later, having traveled from Regina to Calgary to Denver, back to Calgary, again to Denver, then Fort Worth, back to Denver, and finally to Colorado Springs (baggage-handler payback or just plain bad luck).

As Dave told of his latest misfortune, the executives in the audience begin Tweeting about all they were hearing…a cruel customer service incident. The story went viral again as Dave's story resonated this time within the world of Chief Executive Officers in charge of Customer Service. The result should inspire many to trust in extreme heroism and its power to change a world that is so intricately interconnected and instantly accessible through electronic media.

Truth is, injustice does not happen to any of us alone…it often happens to many at the same time…creating similar injustices which add up and create enormous need for someone to respond with extreme heroism. Again United Airlines reached out to Mr. Carroll personally to offer a written apology for his inconveniences and to tell him they wanted "to make this right", thus giving Dave an unusual opportunity…just name what it will take. United Airlines picked up the heroic challenge itself and they began responding with extreme heroism showing that even corporations are teachable and capable of doing the right thing.

Justice restored can be very sweet. United decided to buy and use two of Dave Carroll's videos and last heard was under contract for a third…for United's own customer service training. Dave was reported speaking and performing regularly for major corporations on the importance of client relations.

He responded creatively to an injustice using his own giftedness - special gifts and skills. He did not respond in the old-fashioned way of doing nothing or responding with another injustice. This was extreme heroism or Progressive Art giving birth to words which quickly became melody and lyrics...lyrics and melody became a video....a video connected suffering millions who were set free to advocate according to their own giftedness...and justice being done.

In order that this book be usable as a teaching tool, there is at the conclusion of each story/illustration an analysis which identifies (1) injustice motivating the hero to act and (2) evidence that responses were guided by indiscourageable good will for all involved. For example: **(1) Certain groups of people, often governmental, corporate and bureaucratic, have learned to isolate and insulate themselves from the penalties of doing injustice. They often put people into very helpless positions. (2) Dave's response to an airline's injustice introduces us to the whole new array of responses available through using unique giftedness. The development of social media makes available a whole new category of responses available in today's world that were not available a generation ago.**

* * *

Often our best, most heroic responses to an injustice will be through our strongest and best gifts. That is why the arts are such a rich resource for responding. Artistic painters, crafters, musicians, movie makers, writers, actors, singers and all of us in fact, have some of the resources needed for extreme heroism. We all have within us an instinctive methodology for exposing injustice for the whole world to see.

Extreme Heroism by Song Writers, Singers and Actors

"The hills are alive...with the sound of music!" are the opening words of a famous song from the movie, "Sound of Music" (Wise, 1965), a beloved story of partly fictionalized extreme heroism by a family resisting the growing injustice and rising power of Nazism in pre-world war II Austria. Now, at the beginning of the 21st century, the world still needs the sound of new music as societies continue responding to new forms of injustice. Hopefully the world is better positioned now for the emergence of new heroes from more varied life situations – female heroes and male heroes - child heroes and elderly heroes.

The following are key phrases from three songs from the 1980s which have resonated strongly and powerfully with the public, because as with Dave Carroll, they sing of injustice, injustice well known to everyone and those who respond heroically.

Bonnie Tyler, 1984 and "Holding Out for a Hero"
Shrek II, 2004 and "Holding Out for a Hero"

The first song, "Holding Out for A Hero", was recorded by singer Bonnie Tyler (Pitchford, 1984), in which she sings of a female confined by injustice, crying out urgently for rescue by a male hero and singing, "And it's gotta be soon and he's gotta be larger than life." With this song we have unprecedented opportunity to see an evolution in someone's thought about heroism and where extreme heroes come from. Notice what happens to the meaning of hero in the span of twenty years before "Holding Out for A Hero" reemerges in the animated film, *Shrek II* (Adamson, 2004).

The hero of Tyler's early song, a mere man, has now morphed into a heroic ogre who is considered by the public as the least likely to morph and yet he does. The notion that heroes can come from anyone, regardless of their station in life, is an emerging theme in much 21st century music, which could signal an overall shift toward healthy thinking, especially in the younger generation, about who and what is heroic.

Bette Midler, 1988, Sings of Heroism Overlooked

Actress/singer Bette Midler was elevated in her rise to stardom in 1988 through another song about heroes from the movie, "Beaches"

(Marshall, 1988), entitled "Wind Beneath My Wings" (Selbar, 1988). Bette's character in the movie declares through this song that her best friend, a woman, by then deceased, is a hero. Her lyrics describe a common form of extreme heroism: behind-the-scenes heroism.

Within a week of the movie's release, her words of tribute were on the lips of millions of American and Canadian women who instantly thought of women they knew who had been just like Bette's friend - someone who had facilitated their success by contributing materially and spiritually to their accomplishments without recognition. The music too, becomes a response to an injustice experienced by millions of friends, parents, siblings, strangers, sacrificing heroically without recognition or appreciation.

Funeral directors, pastors and musicians across the continent were soon swamped with requests for "Wind Beneath My Wings" at countless end-of-life remembrances. At first it was women recognizing heroes in other women, but soon it was men and boys celebrating other men and boys...*c*hildhood friends, high school pals, university class mates, army buddies, family members and friends, were being honored all over the continent at funerals as unrecognized heroes were suddenly receiving recognition.

Together the nations have recognized extreme heroism from unexpected parts of life. The song to this day is still a regular part of every funeral home musician's repertoire. Here are just some of those words from the song that lifted so many:

"Did you ever know that you're my hero And
everything I would like to be?"
"I can fly higher than an eagle, For you are the wind beneath my
wings." (Midler, Bette Lyrics Depot www.lyricsdepot.com, 1997)

We might think it hard to find more poignant, heartfelt words than these that recognize the extreme heroes from all our lives, but a mere five years later, in 1993, another singer. Mariah Carey (Carey, 1993) came forth with yet another a hero song, this time about heroes-within. This too was a stunning hit with the American and Canadian public because it celebrated the unsung, unnoticed hero close to home...deep inside. I've been told that Mariah has since declared "Hero" to be her signature song and here are some of the pertinent lyrics:

"There's a hero If you look inside your heart..."
"And you'll finally see the truth...That a hero lies in you"
Hero (Carey, Mariah Lyrics Depot www.lyricsdepot.com, 2004)

Our collective picture of whom and what and where heroes are, is growing larger and becoming clearer by the day. People are becoming bolder and more accurate in their application of the word hero.

In order that this book be usable as a teaching tool, there is at the conclusion of each story/illustration an analysis which identifies (1) injustice motivating the hero to act and (2) evidence that responses were guided by indiscourageable good will for all involved. For example: **(1) Vocalists have had a long and distinguished role in responding to injustices of the human relationship through music whether it's the injustice of unrequited love or the injustice of betrayal or the injustice of divorce. (2) The music and lyrics above refer to the injustice of having no one to rescue us or go with us through the suffering. It's not a response which name names but rather they sing of a predicament or a situation. They are sometimes laments and at other times they are celebrations.**

Extreme Heroism through Poetry & Vaclav Havel

Extreme heroism through poetry is a Progressive Art form and this art form is known for its power to speak clearly and directly to millions of people. At any given moment poetry may be the best of all alternative responses to injustice. Like all Progressive Art it can be quite powerful... consider if you will the Judaic poetry known otherwise as The Psalms (Holy Bible, The New Revised Standard Version, 1997)...all 150 of them written in response to either a national injustice or an individual injustice.

In the March, 2015, issue of "The Atlantic" magazine, an essay on Czechoslovakia's Vaclav Havel and his legacy, by Michael Ignatieff, begins with four 2 1/2-inch-high letters, proclaiming the word HERO. The full context of the title: "The HERO Europe Needed". Ignatieff says in the article, "We tend to think of heroism as mysteriously individual, but Havel's life teaches us that it [heroism] is in fact a social virtue." (Ignatieff, 2015)

Ignatieff elaborates on the heroism he sees in the life of Havel, not as individual super-hero but one of the many and various heroes constantly needed throughout history, rising up to do what they do best as a corporate response to injustice because such responses are "a social virtue". Coincidentally the General Secretary of the United Church of Canada, Nora Sanders, (Sanders, 2015) writing in her Weekly Letter to the denomination, spoke of heroism using similar words when she quoted the church's own "1944 regulation about religious instruction" saying, "Jesus Christ is more than a hero to be admired" to which I would add "more than a hero to be imitated." Jesus' example, like that of Vaclav Havel is to be imitated…each in our own way…according to the injustices in our path and our unique giftedness.

In order that this book be usable as a teaching tool, there is at the conclusion of each story/illustration an analysis which identifies (1) injustice motivating the hero to act and (2) evidence that responses were guided by indiscourageable good will for all involved. For example: **(1) National injustice under a repressive government, like a corporation, isolate and insulate. Political views in these situations can be especially hard to express without being persecuted. (2) Havel responded with poetry. Through poetry he was able to name the injustices he and others saw in Czechoslovakia. Millions read his poetry which the government didn't perceive as a threat, and through sheer numbers of persuaded public opinion reduced the influence of that government until it could be replaced peacefully by another kind of government.**

The Movies as Progressive Art

In recent years, movies as art form, have taken center stage in North America as a heroic tool for exposing injustices for a whole array of people from many different walks life. For example, injustices imposed upon military men and women through war have been exposed in movies like Saving "Private Ryan", "Born on the 4th of July", "Platoon", "Apocalypse Now", "A Band of Brothers", "The Pacific", "Green Zone", "Hurt Locker", "An American Sniper" etc.

Injustices imposed upon individuals and society, by divisions and agencies within our governments, like the Central Intelligence Agency, have been and continue to be exposed through movies like "The Bourne Identity", "The Bourne Supremacy", "The Bourne Ultimatum", "The Bourne Legacy", plus "State of Play", "Body of Lies", "Syriana" and many others. Injustices by charismatic political leaders have been revealed by movies like "Nixon" and "W"; injustices imposed on citizens by corporations like big tobacco in movies like "The Insider" and corporate farming conglomerates in "Michael Clayton"; by nuclear energy and petroleum industry proponents in movies like "The China Syndrome", "Erin Brockovich", "Pelican Brief" et al. The list of products using this powerful, heroic art-form is long.

*****

If you can paint a picture, if you can mold clay, if you can write a song and sing it, if you can create a message in any medium, if you can write a book or poetry, if you can tell a story, if you have good will for others and a sense of injustice and justice, you have an additional means for living extreme heroism and responding appropriately to injustice.

About art, a highly acclaimed Nigerian poet and novelist, Ben Okri (Okri, 2007), has written, "Yes, the highest things are beyond words. That is probably why all art aspires to the condition of wordlessness. When literature works on you, it does so in silence, in your dreams, in your wordless moments."

"Good words enter you and become moods, become the quiet fabric of your being. Like music, like painting, literature too wants to transcend its primary condition and become something higher. Art wants to move into silence, into the emotional and spiritual conditions of the world. Statues become melodies, melodies become yearnings; yearnings become actions."

WORKS CITED

Adamson, A. &. (Director). (2004). *Shrek II* [Motion Picture].

Carey, M. &. (Composer). (1993). Hero. [M. Carey, Performer]

Carey, Mariah Lyrics Depot www.lyricsdepot.com. (2004). Hero.

Davis, A. Y. (2014, Octboer 30). *Sojourners.* Retrieved October 30, 2014, from Verse & Voice: www.sojo.net

Holy Bible, The New Revised Standard Version. (1997). New York: Cambridge University Press.

Ignatieff, M. (2015, March). Atlantic, The. *The Hero Europe Needed,* pp. 96-104.

Lawrence, K. T. (1994). *Imaging the WORD: An Arts and Lectionary Resource.* Cleveland: United Church Press.

Marshall, G. (Director). (1988). *Beaches* [Motion Picture].

Midler, Bette Lyrics Depot www.lyricsdepot.com. (1997). Wind Beneath My Wings.

Okri, B. (2007). *Sojourners.* Retrieved October 6, 2011, from Verse & Voice: www.sojo.net

Pitchford, D. &. (Composer). (1984). Holding Out for A Hero. [B. Tyler, Performer]

Sanders, N. (2015, April 21). General Secretary's Weekly Letter. Toronto, Ontario, Canada: United Church of Canada.

Selbar, J. &. (Composer). (1988). Wind Beneath My Wings. [B. Midlar, Performer]

Sound Track Lyrics www.STLyrics.com. (1984). Holding Out For A Hero.

Wheeler, B. (2009, October 30). *Folk Hero.* Toronto, Ontario, Canada: Globe and Mail Newspaper.

Wise, R. (Director). (1965). *Sound of Music* [Motion Picture].

CHAPTER 13

RESPONDING TO INJUSTICE THRU WHISTLE BLOWING

Introduction to Whistle Blowing

"Whistle Blowing" has become a popular metaphor for an individual who as an insider, takes it upon himself/herself to call others to account for injustices toward one's own family, one's own corporation, one's own colleagues, one's own military unit, one's own classmates, one's own neighbors or any other group to which the whistle blower belongs. It is terribly painful to do because it affects far more than oneself and that is why it ranks as one of the riskiest forms of extreme heroism. Whistle blowing, simply put, is recognizing and exposing an injustice from within…with unrelenting good will, in plain factual language using hard evidence – documents, letters, recordings, videos, etc.

Whistle blowing happens in the nursery when a sibling exposes an injustice by another sibling. It happens in educational settings when a student moves to expose an injustice by another student or by a teacher or professor. It happens in the military when individuals move to expose injustices by other members of their unit.

Indiscourageable good will is essential to making whistle-blowing an act of extreme heroism and cannot be an act of retribution or revenge. In fact, indiscourageable good will in many cases slows the results of whistle-blowing because the victim has good will and hates the possibility of hurting colleagues, military buddies, or family members. Yet communities need to encourage whistle-blowing when it happens, like the young mother writing in her annual Christmas letter to the extended family, reflecting on a 3-year-old son's emergent behavior during the year. As I have said before, she wrote admiringly: "*He really lets us know now when he thinks a family rule has been violated or a family promise has been broken. He holds us accountable and won't let us get away with anything that seems unfair.*"

It is encouraging to see a parent proud of her very own whistle-blower since many parents are inclined to call their whistle-blowers, tattle-tales and teach them "No one likes a tattle-tale and if you want to be liked…don't be a tattle-tale." As we grow older, tattle-tales became "rats" and "snitches". They become, in the eyes of many "despicable"… "scum of the earth" deserving the highest loathing because their actions often expose and lead to losses of power.

Whistle-blowers become material for movies and television. They are the glue that holds organized crime and corrupt policing accountable when no one else can. Even though it is obvious that whistle-blowing is needed and necessary to maintain a justified society, our conditioned aversion to it gets in the way.

In our reluctance to see authorities or institutions as reproachable we teach ourselves to see nothing, say nothing and do nothing…the most primitive of responses. Truth is, the bigger they are the more likely they are to do injustice and then try to cover up. Institutions like the military, the government, business corporations, school boards, universities, pharmaceutical companies, hospitals, banks, insurance companies, stock brokers and the like, simply because they are big means they are likely do some things wrong in a big way and then rely on human reluctance to tattle to keep them from being noticed.

Invariably a person becomes insulated from the truth because no one wants to be labeled a tattle-tale, ostracized or worse. No one wants to risk "spoiling it for everyone else." No one wants to risk costing others part of their financial livelihood.

While the jury is still out on Edward Snowden, former analyst for the National Security Agency, there is much about his story as it comes out that may qualify him some day as legitimate whistle-blower. In the meantime he feels obliged to remain in hiding because he's fearful of government retribution. Heroic whistle-blowing does not expose injustice just for the pleasure of seeing someone 'get caught', but undoubtedly after much prayer and considerable thought. The hero is the one who sees a disastrous result of unabated injustice if he or she doesn't say/do something and out of good will for everyone, devises a strategy or a plan for getting the word out.

They create their own versions of "Deep Throat", a name taken from a story by reporters for The Washington Post who helped Deep Throat expose the misdeeds by the Nixon Administration. Military institutions like the Pentagon, government administrations of which there are many, big oil businesses like Shell, Enron, British-Petroleum and many others; big uranium producers like Kerr-McGee; Big Tobacco; Major Airlines, Giant financial institutions like Chase, Citibank, AIG, Goldman-Sachs and others, because of their size are inherently dangerous to themselves and to the public. They probably don't intend to be that way, but as American Environmentalist Bill McKibben puts it, "In fact, corporations are the infants of our society – they know very little except how to grow (though they're very good at that), and they howl when you set limits. Socializing them" he says, "is the work of politics." (McKibben, 2010)

When politics fail to support whistle-blowing, as it seems to be doing these days, it falls on the rest of us to individually do all we can to re-socialize these big infants with whistle-blowing if necessary before they unintentionally destroy the nation. Big city police departments like those of New York City, Los Angeles, Boston and Chicago, to name just one group, are famous for past corruption lasting for decades because officers couldn't or wouldn't blow the whistle. Imbedded racism among white cops in the 21st century has emerged for people to plainly see, not because of whistle-blowers but because cameras are beginning to expose the cruelty.

Whistle-blowing motivated by good will fits all the parameters of extreme heroism. (1) It means that an injustice has been recognized. (2) It means someone is risking their lives in order to save the lives of others. (3) It means being motivated by wanting the best for everyone involved, i.e. "Friends don't let friends drive drunk," as the slogan goes. Whistle-blowers do not let friends or bosses, addicts, the institutions they work for or those who govern, perpetuate injustice. They find a way to shed light on wrong-doing…guided by good will for all.

The Man Who Couldn't Find His Whistle in Time

It had been a hectic lunch hour down in the canyons…the street-canyons that is, of downtown Dallas, Texas. Trying to get served at their favorite BBQ-stand took longer than usual for two corporate scientists and good friends, Jim and Don. The hubbub was worse than usual that day and it did not dawn on them why, until they had finished their lunch and returned to the busy street outside.

As they emerged from the BBQ joint it finally dawned on them that it was November 20, 1963 and the President of the United States, John F. Kennedy, was scheduled for a visit to Dallas. The street was barricaded to automobile traffic. People were standing eight to ten deep along the sidewalk in every direction for as far as the eye could see, in hopes of seeing the President and First Lady, Jack and Jacque.

Jim and Don felt embarrassed for having forgotten about their visit. Their conversation over root-beer, BBQ beef and beans had not been about politics; it had been about progress they were having in finding new oil and gas reserves. They considered staying to watch the motorcade for a brief moment, but pushing their way through the crowd to the curb to get a view, quickly discouraged them in favor of getting back to the office.

As they moved away from the crowd and the hubbub, things became noticeably quieter and by the time they reached their own office building it was like a Saturday in the canyons, where almost nothing happens in "Big D". They rode the elevators to their office floor and got off. Jim went to his office; Don went to his and was soon deep mentally into his project and therefore startled by ringing of the telephone.

He reached for the phone without taking his eyes off the map he was studying and said "Hello." It was Jim on the phone…shouting! "Don! Are you hearing this?"

"Hearing what?" Don asked.

"The sirens!" he shouted. "Don't you hear the sirens??

"President Kennedy's been shot!"

"No!" said Don pushing back on Jim's words.

He sat deathly still in his chair, not breathing…just listening. Sure enough, he could hear the sirens - sounds of Dallas police and EMTs rushing to help someone, and in this case the sirens seemed like a chorus - a chorus of wailing as those refusing to be comforted.

Jim repeated, "The President's been shot! That's what those sirens are!" He paused and lowered his voice. He said, "I'm coming over to your office. You won't believe what I just heard!"

Don waited and soon heard Jim's footsteps in the hall. The door opened and Jim stepped inside, locking the door behind him. He started right in where they had left off on the phone, almost whispering. "This is unbelievable!" he breathed. "They're now saying the President has been taken to Parkland Hospital and some guy has been arrested already that might have done it!"

Don nodded. Jim sat down and leaned toward Don.

Don said, "You said you heard something!"

Jim: "Yes. You know that report I've been working on?"

"Yes," said Don.

"Well, I actually finished typing it up just before we went to lunch. After we returned, I took it up to management's floor. The boss's office was dark so I thought he and the secretaries were probably still at lunch. The door was unlocked so I let myself in and walked to the secretary's desk to put the report in her in-box.

"It was then that I noticed a light on in the board-room at the far end of the hall. Then I heard voices and the sound of a radio. The door was ajar just enough that I could see some of our management people - six of them maybe – sitting around the table with their shirt-sleeves rolled up, collars open, ties loosened…like they had been there all night. I thought they might be having a working lunch but there was no food…only a radio in the center of the table.

Don thought to himself, wryly, "Yeah, ordinarily they would have been at The Club having prime rib."

"Anyway," Jim said, "the radio was turned up loud enough that I could hear the announcer say, "We interrupt this program to tell you that President Kennedy has been shot just a few moments ago in downtown Dallas as his motorcade was passing by!"

"Get this Don" Jim whispered loudly! They let out a cheer! As if a touch-down had just been scored! Someone at the table said in a loud voice, "We got him!"

"I backed up, ever so quietly, until I reached the door and let myself out. They never knew I was there. That's how I knew the President had been shot and that's when I went to my office and called you."

"Whoa!" Don said. "Whoa!"

They sat quietly for several minutes, the two of them, continuing to listen to the radio and then they heard the voice of famous newscaster Walter Cronkite say, "President Kennedy is dead". Jim had been listening with his head down; his hands folded together. He raised his head and looked at Don and asked, "What should we do?"

Don shook his head and said softly after a pause, "I don't know." A few long moments passed before he said again, "I don't know."

Only later would Don realize what a potent question had been raised, "A great injustice has been done. What should we do?" But for the moment there was only one question he could ask himself, "What the hell is happening?" Although he knew the story, there was the larger question he wasn't ready to entertain. "Did my bosses, the people I'm dependent on for a weekly paycheck, have something to do with the assassination of our President?"

The question was unthinkable a second time. Bosses and corporations for Don were way beyond reproach. The next few hours were a blur. Don had been fond of President Kennedy, even though his time as a soldier in the Far East had been extended. The pain was so great he withdrew into himself and lost interest in his work for the remainder of the day and couldn't function normally.

He finally decided to go home. He caught the elevator, which was empty of the usual folks leaving for the day, down to the street where he walked slowly once more through the empty canyons as darkness was falling. It was several blocks from his office building to where he caught a cross-town bus. The bus too was empty. Don sat staring blindly out the window at familiar streets that he wasn't seeing.

A transformation would occur for Don…a transformation of his understanding of humanity and institutions, what they were capable of, good and bad, but for the moment he wasn't there yet. As night fell he began a vigil in front of the television with millions of others where he slowly accepted the media's suggestion that it was Oswald and Ruby and perhaps Fidel Castro who were to blame. Transformation would have to wait. No heroism on his part…not now.

In order that this book be usable as a teaching tool, there is at the conclusion of each story/illustration an analysis which identifies (1) injustice motivating the hero to act and (2) evidence that responses were guided by indiscourageable good will for all involved. For example: **(1) Injustice within and by organizations are magnified by the size and influence of the organization. Not only is injustice inflicted by the organization but whistle-blowing afflicts the organization itself. Victims often feel trapped in the middle as if biting the hand that feeds them. Passivity is extremely tempting. (2) Don's response is passive but he feels a strong desire to blow the whistle on what could have been a plot against the President of the United States. Press reports quickly dampen his impulses.**

Some of Those Who Found Their Whistles

There are several well documented accounts of that special order of extreme heroes known as whistle blowers...an honorable fraternity:

There is Sharon Watkins - the woman who blew the whistle on the oil company Enron; on good people who did some very bad things with the company pensions and then tried to cover them up – Sharon had been a Vice President – she exposed irregular accounting practices used to defraud employees and deprive them of their life savings.

There was W. Mark Felt – known as Deep Throat - the FBI agent who carefully leaked information to reliable press contacts and through them blew the whistle on the Nixon Administration's illegal involvement in breaking into the Democratic Party Headquarters at Washington's Watergate Hotel – good people doing very bad things in order to get re-elected and keep the power, then trying to cover up.

There was Daniel Elsberg - the man who blew the whistle on the Pentagon's secret pretext for war in Vietnam – good people doing very bad things and then trying to cover them up.

There was Frank Serpico – the policeman who blew the whistle on widespread New York City police corruption – good people doing very bad things and then trying to cover them up.

There was Karen Silkwood – a citizen who exposed deadly safety violations in a nuclear plant in Oklahoma at a time when America was making a major effort to move toward nuclear power as a source of energy – good people doing very bad things and trying to cover them up.

There was Coleen Riley – who revealed FBI inaction and mistakes which may have allowed the 9/11 attacks on New York and the Pentagon to proceed – good people doing very bad things and trying to cover them up.

There was Jeffrey Wigand – he blew the whistle on the tobacco industry – revealing intentional manipulation of nicotine to induce addiction – good people doing very bad things and trying to cover them up.

There was Anita Hill who blew the whistle on Supreme Court Nominee Clarence Thomas for something that would become widely known as sexual harassment. Without realizing it she had inadvertently blown the whistle on all men, white and black, for the sexual liberties, verbally if not also physically, they routinely took with female employees and colleagues.

Several victims of child sexual abuse collectively became whistle-blowers in the Roman Catholic Church, exposing decades of sexual abuse by pedophile priests along with cover-up at the highest levels of the church. The movie "Spotlight" was an Academy Award winner in 2016 for its telling of the collective whistle-blowing done by victims and employees of the Boston Globe News.

These are just a few of those special heroes – whistle-blowers who cared enough about others to say something or do something that would reveal terrible wrong-doing and injustice – friends who wouldn't let friends drive drunk. The risk to these heroes was real; they were almost always discredited, slandered, fired…shamed for "tattling" before they were vindicated.

We must not allow ourselves to think of whistle-blowing as a corporate or institutional response only…an individual versus thousands kind of thing. Whistle-blowing is needed more often between two people… friends not letting friends do things that are harmful to themselves and others. We call it being honest…holding one another accountable… doing those things which will keep smaller things from becoming giant things that are almost too much for one person to speak against.

Marian Wright Edelman, a Children's Rights Activist and recipient of the Presidential Medal of Freedom in 2000, said "You just need to be a flea against injustice. Enough committed fleas biting strategically can make even the biggest dog uncomfortable and transform even the biggest nation." (Edelman, 2007)

WORKS CITED

Edelman, M. W. (2007). *Sojourners*. Retrieved March 13, 2009, from Verse & Voice: www.sojo.net

McKibben, W. E. (2010). *Sojourners*. Retrieved September 10, 2012, from Verse & Voice: www.sojo.net

Oliver, J. (2015, April 6). Host of HBO's "Last Week". (E. Snowden, Interviewee)

CHAPTER 14

EXTREME HEROISM CONTINUES RESPONDING WITH PRAYER

Prayer at the Beginning, Prayer in the Middle, Prayer at the End

I have mentioned prayer before. Extreme heroes go there again and again. It is a beginning place of responses to injustice, it's in all the between places, and it's the concluding place. By the time justice is restored there is a distinct possibility that we will have prayed many times, exposing ourselves to a higher power, whether we refer to it as God, Allah, Yahweh, Buddha, Jesus or simply Creator, Manitou or The Great One. As Sean Caulfield advises in his book "The Experience of Praying", "Sit with God as you might with the ocean. You bring nothing to the ocean, yet it changes you." (Caulfield, 1980)

It is probably never necessary that we recite formal prayers, but some will find that helpful. There are many books on prayer which offer formulaic praying. Others will look for more natural ways of praying...ways that 'feel' right to us in particular...ways that are probably linked closely to the suffering and injustice to which we are responding. Prayer shaped by an injustice, prayer in search of appropriate responses guided by indiscourageable good will are like the air we breathe which we cannot live without.

Responding to injustice by way of the law requires good will combined with prayer to aim at restorative justice, not punitive justice.

Choosing prophetic words in the tradition of Elijah or Mohammed – words with the teeth of a loving parent preserving the lives of her/ his children - requires extraordinary good will, careful thought and prayer to keep them on a path of rescuing, not persecution. Choosing prophetic words in the tradition of Isaiah – words of a feather also require good will, careful thought and prayer.

Choosing word-seeds for planting: stories, parables, allegories, metaphors, poetry - requires unrelenting good will, careful thought and time in prayer. Choosing words consistent with our unique gifts requires good will, careful thought and prayer. Choosing a path to walk when whistle blowing seems our only response to injustice, corporate or one-on-one, requires good will, careful thought and time in prayer.

I for one am praying for an electoral system and process that does not allow the rich to dominate our democracies. For the moment however, I cannot see how our nations can wean themselves from the destructive cycle which has the rich front-loading television with negative campaign advertising which force the poor to fork over their grocery money in order to feed the negative…therefore I pray. I see friends faced with extremely complex challenges for which I see no solutions so prayer for them in their situation is my best response for the moment. Therefore prayer is the beginning place, the in-between place and the ending place.

If the boy on the Big Yellow School Bus knew how to pray – without being taught and without knowing that he knew – then we all know how to pray. Every character in every story in this book has prayed in their own way and perhaps even knew they were praying heroically. Like the other responses to injustice, prayer toward an injustice is extreme heroism.

As Mohandas K. Gandhi put it, "Prayer is not an old woman's idle amusement. Properly understood and applied, it is the most potent instrument of action." (Gandhi, 1945) Gandhi was the preeminent leader of India's independence from British Rule using prayer and other forms of non-violent civil disobedience.

Faced With Injustice Extreme Heroes Know Their Options

Everyone knows how we admonish one another about words-without-actions which make it seem as though we think of words as having no significance. We can't afford to think that way. Words in themselves ARE actions, even the words of prayer and the actions we typically think of as true actions are really the product of the many words that preceded them.

Together there are many options for responding to injustice. No one is ever forced to respond by doing nothing or forced to do violence. There's a time for all of these: The Law as a collection of words arranged in a certain way; prophecy as a collection of words arranged in another way; parabolic teaching which involves additional ways of organizing words for specific purposes; Progressive Art and all those special personal gifts we call aptitudes, skills, abilities and 'giftedness' in writing, music, film-making, sculpture, painting, photography are the actions some look for without realizing those actions are the product and fruit of many carefully chosen words.

We have options. Good options for responding to injustice. The better we know our options the better able we are to live heroically.

WORKS CITED

Caulfield, S. (1980). *The Experience of Praying.* Mahwah: Paulist Press.

Gandhi, M. (1945). *Sojourners.* Retrieved January 12, 2011, from Verse & Voice: www.sojo.net

SECTION III

OBSTACLES, RESTRAINTS, DISCOURAGEMENTS TO EXTREME HEROISM

"Trauma: 1a - a bodily injury caused by a physical force applied from without; 1b–a disordered psychic or behavioral state resulting from stress or injury; 2 a cause of trauma: wound" (Webster's College Dictionary, 2003)

CHAPTER 15

THINGS WHICH ARREST EXTREME HEROISM: TRAUMA

Defining Trauma and the Way It Suppresses Extreme Heroism

The innate human ability to respond to injustice through the indwelling hero, sadly, can be stopped in its tracks by trauma… arrested that is, held hostage, restrained, muzzled, confined, prevented from emerging…unless help arrives. Help may never come because there aren't enough extreme heroes (known in some religious/spiritual circles as reconcilers) trained for responding to injustice. In Christian literature and tradition it was those who had chosen "the way of Jesus" who were declared "reconcilers of the world" believing that everyone could live free and liberated. (II Corinthians 5.18) (Holy Bible, New Revised Standard Version, 1989) I will go out on a limb here and say that most other world religions will have their own names for helpers like these.

A high-school counselor friend of mine once described trauma as "an emotional cave-in"; one that "buries victims alive" and like a physical cave-in, severely limits those areas of life where they can go and function fully and normally. There are multitudes of extreme heroes in this world of ours confined by such cave-ins. Few have any consciousness of their predicament; they just know that sometimes, for reasons they can't understand, that they can't find their voice in time to do anyone any good in the face of injustice.

They often languish, not knowing they are cut off from their own destinies; not knowing whether or not anyone cares enough to come searching for them. The worst offender therefore, standing between heroes and their destinies, are the effects of trauma – extreme bodily and/or emotional shock – a curse that keeps on cursing; paralyzing us with a fear of the trauma repeating itself. Unless relief finally comes their bodies will continually be repressed by anything that reminds them of the circumstances surrounding the original traumatizing event and cease to function.

Trauma in and of itself is a great injustice needing serious and prolonged attention. Trauma limits heroic responses to only a few individuals who happen to share that limited world. Trauma can leave a child or an adult governed indefinitely by these feelings and memories.

A Twelve-Year-Old Girl Traumatized by Poverty & Frontier Life

Janet was a well-balanced 12-year-old girl – very smart and pretty. If she were alive today we would say "there's a girl who has a lot going for her"; "She has it all in terms of physical attributes and personality". None of that would help, however, following Janet's trauma. She lived with her farmer-parents in a remote area of the country during the early 1900s, 60 miles from the nearest town…which was as good as a thousand miles when the only access to civilization was by horseback or horse-drawn wagon.

Thanks to a progressive new government, trying to do something to alleviate widespread poverty along the frontier, a law had been passed called the Homestead Act, through which Janet's parents had been given title to a section of land out west (six-hundred and forty acres). It was theirs to keep if they farmed successfully and made permanent improvements, but the wall between this family and poverty, like it was for many others, was terribly porous. Their survival was dependent totally on the productivity of the land, favorable weather and human cooperation. All these failed Janet.

Janet was typical of 12-year-old girls living far from civilization, seldom seeing other people. She was home-schooled, accustomed to hard work, shy, curious and vulnerable; easily coaxed into a relationship if a rare visitor happened by and made the effort. She helped her mother the way most girls did in those days, learning to cook, sew and clean and then turn to help with the tilling of the land.

Janet still had the unsullied gifts essential to heroism: a keen sense of injustice on the one hand and a keen sense of goodness and fairness on the other, but all that was about to change. Looming on the horizon of this family's future was a severe drought about to drag them further down into poverty along with their neighbors. The drought would set the stage for Janet's crippling trauma.

After a good yield of wheat in the first years, making it possible for the family to picture themselves succeeding at keeping the land, her parents watched with dismay in the following year as the new crops perished from lack of rain. The year recently past would prove to be the last ever, profitable crop. Sensing that the rains might not return in time to help them, many farmers began turning their thoughts to ranching and after months of agonizing over what to do, Janet's father made a special trip to town to withdraw savings from the bank and use it purchase a bull and 6 yearling heifers.

The bull would be used to impregnate the heifers and start a herd. Tying the bull to the family's buckboard wagon, father proudly returned to the farm with a load of supplies, a bull and the six heifers. Word of this spread like wildfire among nearby ranchers who immediately foresaw approaching economic injustice for them if too many people got into the ranching business. To their way of thinking, sodbusters (their word for dehumanizing farmers) had no right to jeopardize the established ranching livelihood.

Their answer to the problem of injustice was to trump the perceived and anticipated injustice with another form of injustice. "If we don't do this," they reasoned, "the sodbusters will only make it harder for the rest of us to survive what they would eventually call "the worst depression the nation has ever known!" Before the month was over, a half-dozen cowhands from a nearby ranch had been dispatched to Janet's farm to "make things right." She was sitting on the dusty front porch just after the noon meal, when the six rode into the front yard.

Father had gone off to tend crops that were over the hill and out of sight. The cowhands had watched and waited until father was gone. Without a word of explanation, they went straight to the corral where they threw a lasso over the new bull. They led it out into the yard and over to the front porch of the house.

Using lassos tied to their saddle horns, with loops tossed around the bull's front and back hooves, they pulled the bull in opposite directions until it fell helplessly to the ground where they castrated it. Janet and her mother watched in horror as Janet became a twelve-year-old arrested hero. The knife of castration cut deeply into her soul as though it had cut her physically and cut into her own family yet unborn.

Many destructive things began to happen to Janet. First, there was a change in the way she thought. It upset the balance between her sensitivity to injustice on the one hand and her sensitivity to goodness and fairness on the other. Her thinking tipped toward injustice until injustice was all she could see.

She developed an exceptionally high sensitivity to unfairness. She became known to her children and grandchildren as "finding fault in everything and everyone", unable to praise or celebrate the good. Only a few discerning people would ever sense the deep, deep fear Janet had of being cut, emotionally.

She couldn't come right out and say, "I'm afraid of castration." All she knew to do was call attention to the slightest injustice that came along.

Secondly, for Janet, there was a change in behavior. She would become anti-social. She narrowed her trust to one or two people at a time. When children were born and growing up, their friends were never welcome in their own home. Her children never knew what birthday parties were and when they finally learned about them they were oddly uncomfortable with them and not likely to host them for their own children.

Janet's children, who often heard the story of their mother's trauma, didn't realize what her story was really telling them…what they needed to know about her, they grew weary of hearing it. The significance of the story, the castration, Momma's trauma, was lost to them. The same thing happened for the grandchildren; they too grew disinterested in going to grandmas' for visits.

When she was finally admitted to the Alzheimer's wing of a nearby assisted living unit, Janet spent her last days telling the castration story to all her nurses and other Alzheimer's patients, seeking with her last breath, apparently, someone who would understand the awful thing had happened to her and her family. No one ever came along who understood, so Janet spent the rest of her life living as best she could in small cramped confines of her tiny "cave". Although there was no mark on her externally, she was nevertheless crippled; capable of extreme heroism at times toward her husband and one or two friends, but otherwise restricted by an invisible vise, unable to respond. Only death would provide an exit.

* * *

Stories like Janet's are not isolated stories by any means. Hers is probably typical of those who experienced the worst of the civil war in the United States or who took part in the settlement of the western frontier. Tommy Lee Jones and Hillary Swank starred in a 2014 movie about that period of time in American history, called "The Homesman" (Jones, 2014). If the movie is unpleasant to watch it's because it's such a real portrayal of life "out west" in a time when many women, to borrow two words from the movie, "went mad".

* * *

The psychological community now recognizes trauma like the one depicted above as something which still commonly occurs throughout

American and Canadian society. Lasting effects of the Great Depression which began in early 1930s have continued into the 21st century.as PTSS or PTSD - Post Traumatic Stress Syndrome or Post Traumatic Stress Disorder. While it happened to Janet and others like her, far from the battlefields of Europe during World War I, no one had a name then for the damage being done to the human psyche on the domestic front by poverty and by the cruelty of next-door neighbors unrestrained by law enforcement. PTSD has continually wreaked havoc on humans and shows signs of getting worse following conflicts in the Middle East, including Iraq and Afghanistan.

Sources of PTSS/PTSD of course are not confined to war. They occur regularly in domestic settings beginning with birth. Following birth there are the challenges of growing up, learning how to socialize in the neighborhood, playground and classroom, getting an education, entering the work force, dealing with divorce, responding to death, unfair job termination, bullying, rape, etc. Trauma producing PTSD occurs frequently as victims become the instruments of traumatizing their own children. It is the domestic equivalent of so-called friendly-fire during combat in which we fire at what seems to be the enemy only to discover that we have wounded one of our own.

Being born into poverty, growing up in poverty, being married and raising a family in a context of poverty…all magnify and multiply the possibilities for crippling trauma. It is always within the best interests of people and government to put an end to poverty. (Plato, 340BCE) Unfortunately legislators and governments are often blind to how urgent the need is and they are reluctant to put the elimination of poverty at the top of their priorities because their affluence blinds them to how deadly poverty can be.

They lose sight of the cost to a nation that comes through trauma not the least of which is suppression of the indwelling hero. Unless we shed light on our traumas and treat them properly, they gradually deaden a nation's heroic responses to injustice. As anti-Nazi dissident and Theologian, Dietrich Bonhoeffer said, in midst of Nazism's rise to power in Germany during the early 1940s, "There remains an experience of incomparable value...to see the great events of world history from below; from the perspective of the outcast, the suspects, the maltreated, the powerless, the oppressed, the reviled – in short, from the perspective of those who suffer – to look with new eyes on matters great and small." (Bonhoeffer, 1963)

WORKS CITED

Bonhoeffer, D. (1963). *The Cost of Discipleship*. New York: Scribners.

Holy Bible, New Revised Standard Version. (1989). Cambridge University Press.

Jones, T. L. (Director). (2014). *The Homesman* [Motion Picture].

Plato. (n.d.). *Verse and Voice*. Retrieved 2010, from Sojourners: www.sojo.net

Webster's College Dictionary. (2003). New York: Barnes & Noble Books.

CHAPTER 16

THINGS WHICH ARREST EXTREME HEROISM: LACK OF "HERO EDUCATION"

Ignorance of Extreme Heroism Arrests the Emergence of Extreme Heroism

Not having a basic understanding of extreme heroism is like not being fluent in a native language and therefore constantly in situations for which there are no words to describe what's going on around us. Without there being a majority of people who have a basic understanding of heroism or its religious/spiritual equivalents there will forever be genuine heroes emerging without the language for understanding or respecting their own behavior in the face of injustice. It is not right that extreme heroism should emerge every day without proper recognition and encouragement in order that there could be a natural progression in the frequency of heroic acts and in the broadened scope of individual heroism among all citizens.

While there are institutions preparing people for a vast array of dangerous vocations, often setting a stage for heroic activity, there is little or no conscious effort to educate or train people in the subject of heroism itself...not in kindergarten, not in elementary school, not in junior high, senior high school, college, nor university. The absence of serious coordinated education leaves learning about heroism and its significance, to chance. So we could leave education where it is and leave it up to the movies and comic books or just plain luck to teach us.

The subject of heroism in a comic book or movie practically guarantees financial success for investors, which is evidence of the widespread interest of the public in the subject, but what the industry teaches often fails to help. Movie and comic book audiences only come away from the experience more likely than ever to see themselves observers of heroes, but not heroes themselves. One could leave hero education to newspapers and television journalists who teach from their own experience; sometimes getting it right and sometimes getting it wrong. There's always the possibility of leaving it to families and friends who teach in the same way, hit and miss, leaving society with a hodgepodge of knowledge about heroism.

Extreme heroes occasionally stand out in a crowd and when that happens it doesn't take long for everyone to reach a consensus that, "Yes, this definitely was heroism." And yet few know exactly how they know that. Intuition seems to tell us when we have witnessed heroism; our 'gut' says its heroism, but one person's hero might be someone else's coward, terrorist, jerk or bully. By the time we graduate from high school our understanding of heroism is likely set for life, shaped by chance, accidents of birth, biases and prejudices of our family and friends, trauma and world events that impinged upon our lives.

Snow boarders, skateboarders, surfers - extreme sports enthusiasts - become heroes in the minds of winter sports enthusiasts because the people they admire constantly risk life and limb for the sake of athletic achievement. Those who want to call that heroism can, but they fail to realize that risk of physical life, is only one part of the equation. Professional football, basketball, hockey players are perceived by some as heroes for the same reasons. Military professionals are heroes to others because of the physical danger they live with on a daily basis.

Law enforcement officials are considered heroes by some, but have proven over the years that they are as vulnerable as anyone to corruption, violence, racism or sexism. Some look to medical professionals for heroism: surgeons, physicians, nurses–depending on how risky we perceive their profession to be. Those who have intimate knowledge about the lives of professional ministers, clergy, priests, imams and rabbis, will eventually perceive that they too are heroes due to the danger inherent in their work. What's often true in all these many walks of life is that the indwelling hero has emerged fully in one professional but not yet fully in another.

One could argue that churches, synagogues, mosques and temples, of all the institutions in our society are the logical ones to educate their members about heroism before sending them into society as practitioners of faith, but experience shows us that this is not happening in religious circles either. So there's a vacuum, a gaping hole in the nation's education system is it pertains to heroism.

It was Martin Luther King, Jr., who said, "The church must be reminded that it is not the master or the servant of the state, but rather the conscience of the state. It must be the guide and the critic of the state, and never its tool. If the church does not recapture its prophetic zeal, it will become an irrelevant social club without moral or spiritual authority." (King, 1965) By abandoning their role as educators of their own, not to mention the general public, religious institutions have sometimes abdicated their role as "conscience of the state" and left extreme heroes as they emerge to fend for themselves.

According to the website of The Pew Center website in Washington, D.C., where there are vast archives of statistics pertaining to politics, social sciences, social issues, religion, technology and global news, there has been no research on heroism. Apparently no one has ever cared enough about heroism to inquire – probably not because they don't recognize heroism but because they think they already know all they need to know about heroism. As Mark Twain once said, "It ain't what you know that gets you into trouble. It's what you know for sure that just ain't so." (Twain 2015)

Real Hero Schools Already

If the nations were to agree that formal heroism education and training were important there would soon be people who could draw up an age-appropriate curriculum on any subject for almost any group of people. A story written by D. Jones in the January, 2009, edition of *Canadian Geographic* tells of a curriculum in Canada that was designed specifically for Search and Rescue Teams (equivalent to civilian Seals or Green Berets, because they bear all the characteristics of extreme heroism. (Jones 2009) The designers didn't come up with the name... Jones did; the founders were simply thinking of the need to have people trained for emergency responses to civilian need; Jones recognized it as a Hero School.

The risk to the lives of students in a school like this is obvious... risk that is mirrored in the risks they will actually have to take in real emergencies across Canada. By providing them with good education and training they have a high chance of succeeding in their heroic endeavors. With a very modest shift in our way of thinking we could imagine many schools, colleges and universities functioning to prepare future extreme heroes.

Police Academies, Military Basic Training Schools, Advanced Military Training Schools, Navy Seals, Green Berets, etc., already exist as models for hero preparation. With appropriate modifications the same schools can prepare students for responding to injustice and doing things inspired by good will for both the perpetrators and victims. Emergency Medical Technician Schools, Nursing Schools, Medical Schools, all train for injustices which have not happened yet; even religious seminaries do that...train for injustices that have yet to happen but will happen to the people to whom they will be called or assigned to; so why not preparation for extreme heroism itself?

CSAR - Canadian Search and Rescue Training (SAR) - a program that includes jumping out of airplanes and rappelling from helicopters in order to respond to the injustice of an injury someone will suffer climbing a mountain or hiking a trail or simply falling, somewhere in one of Canada's national parks or elsewhere in Canada; the injustice of dying in remote locations means needing someone willing to go on a daring rescue mission just to recover someone's remains.

Some of the injustices responded to by CSAR graduates will be accidental and no one's fault; other injustices will be set in motion by the carelessness and recklessness of others; just as it is in the rest of life. CSAR students will learn that most of their responses are already predetermined…meaning they respond with the same good will toward the guilty as they do the innocent in rappelling down a cliff or from a helicopter to perform cardiopulmonary resuscitation, airway management and inserting intravenous lines into a victim's arm. Even though more than half of all SAR assignments turn into body-recovery missions, the SAR Tech motto is defiant: *"That Others May Live"*. If that sounds like extreme heroism, it should.

Here's what one hero said who had joined Canadian Forces in 1987, wistfully comparing his former service in Cold War Europe and Afghanistan to his new vocation in CSAR: "Getting up in the middle of the night to get lowered out of a helicopter and bring somebody back to safety – there aren't many jobs out there like that" (Jones 2009)…a life-giving mission…a life-giving response to an injustice. Not everyone has the physical strength or abilities for responding to injustice this way, but all of us can learn from the CSAR in applying our own gifts and abilities.

In order that this book be usable as a teaching tool, there is at the conclusion of each story/illustration an analysis which identifies (1) injustice motivating the hero to act and (2) evidence that responses were guided by indiscourageable good will for all involved. For example: **(1) Schools, colleges and universities are institutions that anticipate injustice which has not happened yet. They prepare their students in advance for theories and methods for responding to those injustices. (2) Enrolling in these institutions and submitting to the disciplines of learning which they offer is a response to the injustices for which they are designed**

Heroic Curricula

In a perfect world there would be high regard for educating and training for heroism. We would value it highly and make it a top priority, believing that all human beings deserve and need this training. All institutions would deem it sensible to design curriculum. Even religious institutions would be willing to design heroism curriculum for pre-school, elementary, junior high and high school age children. In a perfect world we would also design catch-up courses for older generations who never had formal training in heroism. The following are just a few curriculum suggestions:

At the Beginning Know What Makes Extreme Heroism Extreme

By definition all forms of heroism are risky and self-sacrificing...one can be hurt, injured or even killed responding heroically. It was G. K. Chesterton (Chesterton n.d.) who said "Jesus promised his disciples three things: that they would be completely fearless, absurdly happy, and in constant trouble." Extreme heroism does lead in each of those directions simultaneously…the absence of fear, absurd happiness and constant risk of losing some form of our own life for the sake of increased life for others.

Question One: Name the four dimensions in which one can be hurt, injured or killed when responding heroically.

<u>Answer</u>: ***physical*** (hurt, injury or death to one's body); ***emotional*** (hurt, injury or trauma) to one's emotions; ***mental*** (hurt, injury or trauma) to one's mind; ***spiritual*** (hurt, injury, trauma) to one's spirit/soul.

* * *

Question Two: In addition to risk and self-sacrifice and the four ways one can be hurt, injured or killed; **name <u>two other criteria</u> essential to qualifying an act as extreme heroism:**

Answer 1: By definition extreme heroism always **responds to injustice (something unfair or wrong)**. If there is no apparent injustice involved in a situation that is risky and dangerous then that act may qualify as heroism to some but not as extreme heroism (i.e. skate-boarding, mountain-climbing)

Answer 2: By definition extreme heroism always strives to respond to an injustice out of a strong sense of **good will for both victims and perpetrators**. (A response born of good will for the victim ***only*** is more likely to produce another injustice.) As difficult as it may be to do, a response born from good will for both sides is more likely to restore justice, fairness and right relationships.

True or False Questions About Extreme Heroism

True or False: Extreme heroism is primarily the domain of males.

Answer: False. Heroism has never been the exclusive domain of males. Hurt, injury and death can occur emotionally, mentally, spiritually and physically to females as well as males. The Greek culture which practically invented the concept of heroism 3000 years ago wrote of and spoke of both their female and male heroes. In Christianity women were clearly recognized as ‘ιεροσ/ heroes from the first century onward during which ‘ιεροσ was simply translated as priest and saint.

True or False: Extreme heroism is limited to Young Adults/Middle Age; 20-50.

Answer: False. Because extreme heroism is essentially part of our genetic make-up...our DNA...that heroic impulse can and does emerge at every age. Children exhibit heroic responses to injustice and so do the elderly. The ability to be hurt, injured or ‘killed’ is present at every age and doesn’t become dormant because we are younger or go away because we are older. The worst that can happen is the heroic impulse being discouraged, squelched or beaten into submission.

True or False: Extreme heroism is confined largely to combat during wartime.

Answer: False. This was widely accepted up through the mid-1900s because war had so dominated the human experience in Europe and North America, but while war presented many opportunities for extreme heroism within a wartime context, in truth it was not the only context in which men, women and children could respond heroically. Since the mid-1900s the ingredients of risk and danger and therefore opportunities for heroism have been recognized in countless domestic fronts: nurseries, marriage, schools, neighborhoods, businesses and in countless professions: medicine, parenting, teaching, search and rescue and law enforcement.

True or False: While heroism is a concept common to many languages: Greek, Italian, Spanish, Portuguese, French and English, the word hero and its derivatives do not appear in the English translations of the sacred literature of Christians.

Answer: True. The One-Volume Exhaustive Concordance of the Bible (Interpreter's One-Volume Commentary on the Bible 1971) does not list the word hero or any of its English derivatives.

True or False: Heroism was a concept familiar to the Greek culture in which Christianity found its roots through Jesus of Nazareth. In fact these concepts dominated that culture.

Answer: True. Jesus did not openly oppose these concepts but pioneered in claiming what I have herein called extreme heroism. Extreme heroism is the jurisdiction of everyone, beginning with the least, the poor, children, elderly, women, the uneducated, strangers and outcast; the marginalized. Everyone was born with the same "hero stuff" residing within.

True or False: Heroism is taught in many places: churches, synagogues, mosques…pre-school, elementary school, junior high and high school, college, universities. Everyone in North America has pretty much the same understanding of heroism.

Answer: False. While the word heroism is a common part of our North American vocabulary it is not formally taught by that name. Most churches do not think of it as their domain or shy away from it. School systems do not teach heroism. Our understanding of heroism is therefore quite varied. What we have learned about heroism we have gleaned from conversations with peers, from reading comic books, viewing movies and video games. Seldom is heroism thought of as a response to injustice nor is it seen as a beneficial gesture toward perpetrators as well as victims.

True or False: Heroism is generally thought of as something everyone can do.

Answer: False. Left to our own resources we are more likely to think of heroism as 1st Century Greeks thought of it…a phenomenon among the super-human, exceptionally gifted people.

Profiling Our Personal Responses to Injustice

Here is an opportunity to be honest and objective about your own personal response profile to injustice. Answer each of the questions below in order to develop a profile of your personal history and your probable response in most cases of injustice.

Question 1: There are nine major ways to respond to an injustice: (1) Pray, (2) Do and Say Nothing, (3) Respond with Violence, (4) Legal Response, (5) Verbal Response A (early prophetic), (6) Verbal Response B (late prophetic), (7) Verbal Response C – parable, poem, story, et al, (8) Artistic Responses, (9) Whistle Blower Response, (10) Prayer. Given your personal history…the types of responses you observed in those around you when you were a child…the types of responses you seem to favor now…what does this suggest you would probably do, without further education and training, when the next injustice occurs in your life.

Question 2: Injustices are likely to occur in our (1) domestic relationships (family, friendship, marriage), (2) professional relationships (colleagues, administrators), (3) government relationships (taxation, benefits, border crossings), (4) neighbor-hood relationships, (5) church relationships, and (6) community relationships (social issues and needs). Which of these relationship sets are more likely to present you with injustice in the next 10 years?

Question 3: What is the earliest injustice you can remember facing? Which of the nine major ways did you use in responding?

Question 4: What was the next injustice you faced? Which of the nine major ways did you use in responding? Were you aware that it was unjust and that there were appropriate things you could do about that injustice? Were you aware at the time of the importance of good will for yourself? Others, victims, perpetrators?

Question 5: What do you believe about the power of words to change things? What do you think of the power of 'strong' words versus the power of 'gentle words'? What do you think of 'negative' words as opposed to the power of 'optimistic' words? What do you think of 'hopeful' words as opposed to the power of pessimism and sarcasm?

Question 6: Beyond your words, talk about your personal giftedness for responding to injustice (art, music, knitting, sewing, repairing, fixing, creating, making movies, etc.).

Question 7: Talk about Edward Snowden, former NSA employee in the U.S. Does he qualify more as a 'whistleblower' or a 'traitor'? Have you ever been a whistleblower? Share an experience.

(Military Security…while on special assignment in Seoul, South Korea, several fellow soldiers walked off the job and failed to appear for duty the next day. They went out "on the town" leaving others forced to cover for them and stay on duty for the rest of the night. The incident was reported to the commanding officer. The offenders were reprimanded and demoted. Problem: If this was reported out of spite or revenge would it be extreme heroism? (Answer: No, although this was a form of desertion which could get soldiers killed, there would be no point in revenge.) If this were a reasoned response with no ill will intended but with a view toward better Army Security would it qualify as extreme heroism? (Answer: Yes.)

Question 8: Talk about an artistic/creative response you've used in responding to an injustice. Was it a poem, a parable or story? What was the injustice and what did you do?

<u>Question 9</u>: So where do you exist on the good will spectrum? Is EH (extreme heroism) something we distrust or is it something we embrace? Is it something we turn on and off...depending...or is it something we turn on and leave in the on position? Do we employ good will for victims but not perpetrators? Do we consciously seek the guidance of good will in deciding how to respond to the injustices encountered in our lives?

Practice Discerning Extreme Heroism

In the Prologue, the story of Paul at the crash site (p. iv-ix). (1) What was the injustice to which Paul was responding? Do you think he thought of it as an injustice? Or is it likely that he simply responded to the needs he saw? (2) What evidence was there that Paul was responding with indiscourageable good will? (3) What was there about Paul that might have disqualified him as an extreme hero to an outsider watching the whole thing happen? What was the risk involved with his decision to rescue and care for the others?

An Exercise in Identifying an Injustice: From Pain to Witness

Assuming that everyone, even the super-rich, has within them a spirit of extreme heroism it is worth encouraging that spirit to speak...speak of the injustice it already knows. It may be local injustice...something seen every day and/or it may be personal injustice...something felt every day and largely unknown to others; it may be injustice reported from around the world. Whether local or personal or on a world scale, injustice is something we can't get off our minds...so let's do as Debbie Deane suggested, (Deane, 2011) "...bear witness to it".

It will arouse strong feelings within us as we remember and even stronger feelings as we move toward a response, perhaps it began with private grumbling to a close friend or a letter written to the editor of a local newspaper. When we are satisfied that we have identified and clearly defined that injustice, then describe it...thoroughly exhaust your vocabulary in describing it and naming it. Once that's been done, turn to describing what life would be like without that injustice...thoroughly exhaust your vocabulary again in describing the justice you would like to see take its place. Then be prepared at some point to repeat the whole process with one or more others.

By the time you have done these things, options for responding will have crept into your consciousness. Give yourself opportunity for complete catharsis by capturing some of them; get them all out; your thoughts and feelings about the injustice; your thoughts and feelings about the justice to come and the ways by which it might happen. If your response has been measured sufficiently by good will and can be done alone, then do it alone. If your response needs to be shared by one others, then by all means, recruit them, continuing all the while, measuring your response by good will, and then gather the others together and do it.

Teaching As a Response to Injustice

If we can agree that an injustice is done by not-teaching heroism (which includes extreme heroism) then the logical response will be to teach, but as soon as we agree that heroism is worthy of teaching we will have to decide on whose shoulders the task of teaching extreme heroism should rest. Perhaps the responsibility should rest with the religious community, but historically that community has given it a pass. Perhaps the responsibility should rest with public education...perhaps the responsibility can be shouldered by both.

Whoever teaches future generations about extreme heroism will have to decide at what age we can teach it. It would seem that sooner is better than later...certainly by the time we enter elementary school when children are most likely to be subjected to the injustice of bullying. Having said this it even makes sense that heroism be taught at every age, at least as younger children transition to older elementary, junior high school, high school; even at university levels the many refresher courses along the way would seem appropriate.

Someone needs to step up and do the right thing for the people beyond their own circles of heroism. It is not enough to teach only our own. Cynthia Bourgeault, an American Episcopal priest said, “What is missing in Christianity is the real understanding that practice doesn't just mean people going inward to do their own little spiritual trip. It is a way of re-patterning the whole physical, neurological, emotional, devotional animal so that it understands what it is doing." (Bourgeault, 2012) As an extreme hero...know what you're doing, even as you do it.

BIBLIOGRAPHY

Bourgeault, Cynthia Rev. Dr. *Sojourners.* 2012. www.sojo.net (accessed January 14, 2014).

Chesterton, G. K. n.d. Sojourners sojo.net (accessed March 03, 2016).

Deane, Debbie H. *Verse and Voice.* 2011. www.sojo.net (accessed 2011).

Interpreter's One-Volume Commentary on the Bible. Nashville: Abingdon Press, 1971.

Jones, Deborah. "Hero School." *Canadian Geographic.* January/February 2009.

King, Jr., Martin Luther. *Sojourners.* 1965. www.sojo.net (accessed September 18, 2006).

Twain, Mark. *Desk Calendar.* April 22, 2015.

CHAPTER 17

THINGS WHICH ARREST EXTREME HEROISM: BULLYING

Bullying, Childhood Violence and Trauma

Bullying is a form of violence often associated with childhood and the teen years where one child or youth feels compelled at very least to intimidate another child with the threat of physical injury, embarrassment or deprivation which may lead to actual injury, shame or loss. Carrying out these threats is usually done alone, in private, or with one or two companions who observe and thereby enhance the bully's pleasure. Some bullies as they grow older continue bullying privately and publicly.

On the face of it, bullying is a peculiar, odd response to another person's peculiarities, shyness or reticence. Apparently all of those behaviors signal weakness and vulnerability to the bully and for some reason make the bully feel uncomfortable. In order to escape his/her discomfort the bully feels compelled to respond with various forms of intimidation.

Obviously bullying is not confined to childhood unless it is halted there, but unless halted, childhood bullies become adulthood bullies. Bullying perpetually leads to crippling trauma in the victim (see Ch. 15). Over time, repeated bullying by parents or anyone in authority can lead to trauma as powerful as one single event. Some parents bully their own children and think they are parenting.

Some people bully their spouses; many employers bully their employees; some colleagues bully other colleagues. Adult bullying is as common as childhood bullying but with higher stakes. The more radical bullying is done behind the scenes when no one is looking, making it hard to prove. It isolates victims and renders potential heroes impotent.

Bullying pervades politics, government, business, and sometimes religious institutions. It exists even in well-established democracies. As it approaches domination it comes close to being criminal. A U.S. governor/presidential candidate has been under indictment for bullying a state district attorney; another U.S. governor has been under investigation for bullying a small town mayor. Bullying at the higher levels is better known as corruption.

Bullying is part of every culture. Historically, like other bad human behavior it has often been dismissed as something every generation has to live with…meaning, tolerate…put up with. We've heard it said that we can "chalk it up to boys being boys", "girls being girls" or "people biologically wired that way". Most people feel helpless to do anything about bullying when they are victims of it.

Nowadays, with the advent of the internet, bullying has found new fertile ground for its secretive, clandestine activities, but along with that has come greater public awareness. The internet and features like Twitter have made bullying easier and more tempting. With awareness there is now less willingness to simply accept bullying as something we have to live with and more effort is being made to stop it during childhood.

Starvin' Marvin the Rodeo Clown

After decades of tolerance to bullying, schools in the U.S. and Canada have been responding to bullying in grade school and high school… going so far as introducing anti-bullying programs as part of the education curriculum. People in some western states for example, have come to know the name of *Starvin' Marvin*, who seems as a rodeo clown to be an unlikely hero, but he has been responding to injustice out of his own giftedness (see Ch. 12), knowledge of bulls and broncs, cowboys and cowgirls. His friends know him as Marvin Nash (Nash, 2010), "the man who is pioneering efforts to assist teenage victims of bullying".

Marvin rolled his rodeo barrel, his only means of protection as a rodeo clown, all the way from Wyoming to Washington, D.C. where he appeared before the United States Senate, in order to underscore the problem of bullying all across the nation. He told the Senate "Every day 160,000 kids don't go to school because they're afraid of being bullied." He told reporters that he felt compelled to do something for kids and out of his 44 years as a rodeo clown, protecting cowboys from 2000 pound bulls, he found that he could protect children from the "bull" in bullying.

Marvin may not have intended his work protecting cowboys from bulls to become a metaphor for what he really deems important, but it is a fair comparison that the words 'bully' and "bull" have the same root. His mission has shifted to protecting kids from the weight of bullying. The Casper Star Tribune reported September 3, 2010 (Borchardt, Jackie), that five schools in the Natrona County District were going to give Marvin's program, "Bullying Hurts" a try.

By the time this was inaugurated there were already three hundred organizations in the United States and thirty-two States where similar programs were underway. It's a late start on the problem...kind of surprising that we didn't realize sooner how damaging this was to our children. Now that we ARE becoming aware we can see how important it is to disrupt the bullying cycle, rescue victims AND perpetrators from limited, restricted lives.

We also live in a time when girls have become more frequent targets for bullying, through cyber-bullying – bullying through the internet. Schools are finally offering opportunities to girls and boys for recognizing that the bullying happening to them is NOT normal and therefore not acceptable. Students are being taught effective responses to make.

In some cases older students - victims themselves at an earlier age - are being taught to mentor others and provide safety on the way to and from school and in school cafeterias at lunch time. At the same time, those who bully are being targeted with programs designed to focus attention on them and their behaviors toward other students, defining it not only as NOT cool but deserving penalties.

Keys to Ending Bullying

Behold the evidence that some things are changing for the better: Although bullying has been around since the serpent first bullied Eve in the Garden of Eden and although most of us have experienced bullying, we are only just now in the 21st century acquiring a vocabulary for those experiences. While bullying is as common as dirt we simply didn't have a name for it so we never learned to put the experience and the word bully together. Now see how far we have come.

It means there is hope for the flowers…hope for budding extreme heroes to come alive and rise up to assert their heroism. Thanks to Greater Good Magazine who recently published excerpts from a book by Signe Whitson (Whitson, 2014), we have a glimpse into what people are saying about bullying in 2014…that it can be put to an end. Her article was entitled, "Eight Keys to End Bullying": (1) Know bullying when you see it; (2) Establish connections with kids; (3) Stop bullying whenever you see it; (4) Deal directly with cyber-bullying; (5) Build social and emotional skills for both bullies and victims; (6) Turn bystanders into buddies; (7) Reach out to kids who bully; and (8) Keep the conversation going. More about her book can be seen on Signe's website (www.signewhitson.com).

Bully Parents Bullied Themselves as Children

Tim was severely bullied as a child by his mother. She would have been mortified had she known that what she thought was good parenting, just parenting the way she had been parented, was actually bullying and not parenting at all. Tim's memories of growing up were largely of his mother's face twisted with anger, demanding that he conform to her way of thinking. With that came the perpetual threat of disapproval and the withholding of love and affection.

Tim was thoroughly traumatized by the bullying by time he was six years old. The abuse continued through elementary school, high school and so long as he was living at home…even into college. It was always done in private…after school and before Tim's Dad got home from work.

Tim came to know his mother as two people…the one who bullied him when no one else was looking or listening and the one who was personable, sweet and gracious when others were present. He often puzzled over the person who met guests and complete strangers with such accord and the person who almost never treated him the same way. Tim's mother was 102 when she died…bullying had not kept her from having a long life…but she never stopped bullying her son either. Just…couldn't help it…couldn't give it up…as though it were her right.

To her of course it wasn't bullying…she would have called it mothering…a role which she treasured and compulsively maintained toward Tim until the very end. They were never, ever to be equals… two adults who could converse, exchange ideas and have cordial disagreements. She couldn't bring herself to be submissive to Tim in any way, like learning what Tim might have learned while away at school for the day or the semester or at his work…needing always to 'lord it over him'.

After intensive counseling and therapy Tim was able to see clearly his mother's influence and that he had been following in her path. It took years to undo but he was able to move on to a different relationship with his own children. He learned the virtues and the joys of meeting them on a level playing field where he was equal, not superior, not less than them but always a contributor to their lives.

Unchecked bullying in childhood and the teen years goes on to become bullying in adulthood. It is a way of life for many adults, still hidden and transacted in secret…a corrupting influence for people from all walks of life. It was Cesar Chavez, a prominent civil rights activist among American farm workers and recipient of the Presidential Medal of Freedom, who said of children, "Perhaps we can bring the day when children will learn from their earliest days that being fully man and fully woman means to give one's life to the liberation of the brother who suffers [i.e. extreme heroism]." (Chavez, 2009)

In our indiscourageable good will for children, let us remember to have indiscourageable good will for those who mother them as they themselves were mothered. They need to understand why they are alone in their old age in the same way an alcoholic needs to understand why they too are all alone. We need programs for them as ambitious as those we are building for children and that's not impossible, just challenging.

Those who bullied in the name of mothering or fathering need to make use of the time they have remaining in this life to give their adult children as many memories as possible of their parent's sometimes obscure ability to care and to love with a love they've always been capable of. It was African American poet and another recipient of the Presidential Medal of Freedom, Maya Angelou, who wrote, "I've learned that people will forget what you said, people will [even] forget what you did, but people will never forget how you made them feel." (Angelou, 2013) Please, please, please…let us remember our dual obligation to the perpetrators as well as the victims, to do all we can, in the time left, to leave these child-parents feeling joy: feeling good about themselves, good about others and, if they believe in God…feeling good about God…all at the same time.

WORKS CITED

Angelou, M. (2013). *Good Reads*. Retrieved April 28, 2015, from goodreads.com: http://goodreads.com/quotes/5934-I-learned-that-people

Borchardt, Jackie. (2010, September 3). High School Students teach anti-bullying program. Casper, WY, US: Casper Star-Tribune.

Chavez, C. (2009, April 26). Retrieved April 28, 2015, from National Farm Worker Ministry: www://nfwm.org/2009/04/quotesfromcesarchavez

Nash, M. (2010, July 20). Bullying Hurts Program. (P. Dvorak, Interviewer)

Whitson, S. (2014, August 26). *Greater Good Magazine*. Retrieved April 28, 2015, from Greater Good Magazine: www.greatergood.berkeley.edu/article/item/eight_keys_to_end_bullying

CHAPTER 18

THINGS WHICH ARREST EXTREME HEROISM: HABIT

Habits Can Be Habit-Forming

Any time we set out to break our own destructive habits we need to be reminded of just how powerful habit can be in suppressing extreme heroism. Good intentions are often no match for strong habits like passivity or violence. Such habits can be habit-forming.

Underneath it all we ARE extreme heroes but until we get a taste of doing extreme heroism and know that we do not have to stop at one act of heroism, extreme heroism can be overcome by the emotional inertia of our former lives. Until we realize that extreme heroes do not have to perform attention-getting acts of heroism with every breath and know that tiny acts of extreme heroism are as effective as attention-getting-heroism, we are prone to be creatures of habit and nothing will be new under the sun. If we learn passive responses to injustice in childhood we are quite likely to continue passive responses all of our life...out of habit. . .unless or until a severe injustice snaps us out of our hypnotic fog.

If we learn violent aggressive responses to injustice in early childhood we are quite likely to continue violent aggressive responses into adulthood...out of habit. . .unless or until we become victims of an injustice which propels us toward some alternative response. Habit has the deadly effect of inhibiting and delaying good responses to injustice until or unless something derails or distracts. The religious faithful who gather routinely for worship, organized prayer and other rituals, are as vulnerable as anyone to habits dulling their sensitivity to injustice. Habit can have a numbing effect which keeps us from responding to injustice even in our closest relationships.

Habit and affluence work together to compound and postpone extreme heroism. With unlimited financial resources where there is no end to ways to spend money on ourselves we can remain blinded indefinitely to the desperate need of others. It was Jose Marti, a Cuban national hero, poet, journalist and revolutionary philosopher who said, "Habit creates the appearance of justice; progress has no greater enemy than habit." (Marti, 1890)

WORKS CITED

Marti, J. (1890). *izquotes*. Retrieved April 2015, 2015, from izquotes: www.izquotes.com/quote/315965

SECTION IV

EXTREME HEROISM: THE WHOLE THING

CHAPTER 19

HEROISM: THE ONE THING WITHIN THE WHOLE THING

First There's Extreme Heroism…And Then There's All the Rest

You know the saying, "Beauty is in the eye of the beholder." Likewise, "Heroism is in the eye of the beholder." No one it seems, can say with certainty, "This is heroism and the other is not."

Extreme heroism on the other hand, can be defined simply as responding to an injustice with a view to making things right again guided by indiscourageable good will for both victims of injustice and perpetrators of injustice. Seekers of truth about these matters must weigh the evidence, identify the injustice and evaluate the response before declaring one way or another that an act is extreme heroism or another form of heroism. On the one hand we have extreme heroism and on the other hand we have all the rest of heroism…everything that remains if we subtract extreme heroism, which is a lot.

All the remaining heroism in the world may be heroism from which the ancients tried to distance themselves by selecting other words, like saint, priest, holy or even "the way…the truth…and the life". (Holy Bible, The New Revised Standard Version, 1997). Perhaps they wanted to discredit heroism as they had known it so that their friends could avoid associating with it altogether. Maybe they were correct in thinking that their generation was incapable of navigating through all conventional thought on heroism and still arrive at indiscourageable good will for all.

Perhaps also they were afraid their descendants would be tempted to eliminate legitimate examples of extreme heroism because of age… considering some too young or too old for extreme heroism. Perhaps they were afraid of extreme heroism being thought accessible only to the physically strong; worse, only the super-gifted. Perhaps they were afraid they would be tempted to eliminate extreme heroes because of gender or lack of education or social/economic status.

Meanwhile, centuries have passed and extreme heroism has continued emerging in every part of humanity on earth. It is now called by other names in various religions and cultures, emerging repeatedly; doesn't seem to matter whether people speak English or Russian, French or Arabic or some other language. Extraordinary heroes came out of the Independence movement of India from the United Kingdom in 1940s; through the Civil Rights Movement in the United States which emerged in the 1960s; through the Anti-Apartheid Movement in South Africa in the 1990s; through the Same-Sex Marriage Act in Canada [first of its kind outside of Europe] in 2005 (Wikipedia, 2010) and Canada's Truth & Reconciliation Conferences in 2010 for the sake of Aboriginal people of Canada (Centre, 2010).

As more and more heroes have emerged among English speaking people we find them turning more and more to hero vocabulary to describe things going on in their lives. Hero sightings seem to be increasing. Christians are no longer the only ones needing words like priestly, saintly, holy or "the way" to describe the things that are happening.

Diane Nash, an organizer of Freedom Rides during the Civil Rights Movement seemed to be thinking of extreme heroism when she wrote "The movement had a way of reaching inside me and bringing out things that I never knew were there, like courage and love for people. It was a real experience to be seeing a group of people who would put their bodies between you and danger. And to love people that you work with enough that you would put your body between them and danger." (Nash, 1962)

As I look ahead to the things which might happen during our life-times, because we embraced the concept of extreme heroism, I remember Frederick Buechner's words from his book "Whispering in the Dark". He was a Presbyterian minister, writer and theologian who never pastored a church and rarely attended worship, but seemed to have had a keen appreciation of extreme heroism. Whether he called it that or not isn't important. He described it, however, in his own words as an extraordinary thing and he wrote: "The extraordinary thing that is about to happen is matched only by the extraordinary moment just before it happens. Advent is the name of that moment." (Buechner, 1993)

Advent comes to prepare us for the effects of extreme heroism. Those living through this beginning of the 21st Century are living through an "Advent time"...that extraordinary moment of Buechner that comes just before another extraordinary thing happens. This may become a time in which it will be said the people embraced their own extreme heroism and rose bravely and lovingly to meet the many occasions set before them.

WORKS CITED

Buechner, F. (1993). *Whistling in the Dark: A Doubter's Dictionary.* San Francisco: HarperCollins.

Centre, C. N. (2010). Truth and Reconciliation Conferences. Winnipeg, Manitoba, Canada.

Holy Bible, The New Revised Standard Version. (1997). New York: Cambridge University Press.

Nash, D. (1962). *Sojourners.* Retrieved March 25, 2010, from Verse & Voice: www.sojo.net

Wikipedia. (2010). *Wikipedia.* Retrieved May 1, 2015, from Wikipedia: www.wikipedia.org

CHAPTER 20

EXTREME HEROISM AND INDISCOURAGEABLE GOOD WILL

In Chapter 1 it was asserted that extreme heroism is inseparable from injustice, but with every injustice and response there is one other thing that makes extreme heroism extreme. It's called indiscourageable good will...wanting the best for enemies as well as friends. These two things set extreme heroism apart from all other forms of heroism.

A Doctor That Still Made House Calls

The word "indiscourageable" will not be found in most dictionaries. It should be, but isn't. True, there are synonyms for indiscourageable, like unrelenting, unwavering and steadfast, but I prefer indiscourageable because it admits to the potential for being discouraged while trying to have good will toward (1) a creator whose presence is sometimes hard to discern, (2) our neighbors or ourselves for behaving badly, and (3) toward our enemies, real or perceived. I owe the concept of indiscourageable good will to a former family physician and one of my early adult spiritual leaders, Dr. Jimmy Barnard (Barnard, 1965) who actually made, what was considered, even 50 years ago, a rare house-call to attend to my child's illness even as palm trees were being ripped from their roots and strewn across rooftops and streets at the height of a brutal hurricane making a direct hit on Corpus Christi, Texas.

I have since come to believe that anything less than indiscourageable good will thrusts our responses to injustice to some other part of the heroic continuum. While there is risk and danger in all parts of the spectrum, risk and danger alone do not make for extreme heroism. Wanting the best for everyone in the face of injustice, for both victim and perpetrator, is what makes it extreme; a stance that can be a difficult to come to and even harder to maintain.

Dr. Jimmy, as we called him, often shared with his adult Sunday School Class his personal experiences in applying indiscourageable good will, or what he sometimes called godly love, during his tenure as Mayor of Corpus Christi. He was quick to stress that having such an attitude did not mean having affection or liking for everyone nor did it exclude having great anger toward some at times. It simply meant being vigilant for ways that his actions might prove beneficial to enemies and victims, in the same way black communities in the U.S. under the leadership of Rev. Dr. Martin Luther King, Jr., looked to benefit both the black and white communities by their actions.

Indiscourageable Good Will and the Color Purple

In watching the 1985 movie, The Color Purple, (Spielberg, 1985) based on a book by Alice Walker, the viewer meets the long-suffering and victimized wife, Celie, whom our hearts go out to, played by Whoopi Goldberg; and her movie husband, the villainous sharecropper, Albert, played by Danny Glover, a character he made easy to loathe and hate. Good will for the latter becomes unthinkable after the audience sees a lonely Celie writing tearful letters to her sister and confidant Nettie, gone away to find her fortune in Africa, with Albert cruelly hiding those letters instead of mailing them, partly because he's jealous of the sister's love for one another. Years pass as Celie assumes her sister has died.

When she finds the stash of unsent letters and realizes what Albert has NOT done over the years, she finds her voice and the courage to finally stand up to him and leave him, in order to find a life apart from him (a form of extreme heroism recognized by the Alcoholics Anonymous program called *detachment with love*). Thanks to Alice Walker's insight the viewers and readers are surprised when they find themselves feeling good will toward Albert who responds to Celie's courageous departure by finally sending the letters to Nettie that he should have sent years earlier. The letters find Nettie still alive and thriving in Africa.

She responds to the letters by returning to America where she and Celie are reunited and the movie ends with Albert being redeemed although alone, out plowing his fields in the warmth of a setting sun. Thanks to Alice Walker and director Steven Spielberg, the audience is allowed to see the good in both perpetrator and victim as if to suggest that the universe, higher power, God or Allah wants things to turn out good for both. These two things then: (1) injustice followed by (2) responses guided by indiscourageable good will…are the things that keep heroes at the extreme part of the heroic spectrum, actually changing the world for the better and which, much to everyone's surprise, actually falls within the scope of every human's capability.

A 91-Year-Old Canadian Hero, Ed Carter-Edwards

It's never too late for an elderly woman or man to act out of indiscourageable good will, even for those hard to love. Even their last breath can be inseparable from acts of extreme heroism, yet the good will is a concept hard to embrace for many people. Getting there always raises questions about good will for those who are the hardest to love, so that the question most asked about indiscourageable good will is "Does this apply to someone like Adolf Hitler whose leadership in Germany led to such unspeakable crimes against humanity in World War II?"

Ed Carter-Edwards, a 91-year-old Canadian veteran of World-War-II, recently provided his answer to that question when he returned to Europe for VE Day, 2015, (Victory in Europe Day) to pay a visit to the Nazi death camp at Buchenwald, near Weimar, Germany, where he had been held prisoner until the allied forces liberated France in 1941. Ed had been a member of the Royal Canadian Air Force and was on his 22nd mission when shot down over occupied France. Eventually his French captors turned him over to the Gestapo who sent him to Buchenwald along with 167 other airmen, presumably to work, be executed and cremated along with the Jews.

Ed's unique perspective as a Canadian shot out of the sky after 22 successful missions, thrust him directly and suddenly into the heart of the horror, forcing him to see in an instant what the Nazis were doing to everyone who didn't align themselves correctly. His experience illustrates dramatically how hard it is to have indiscourageable good will for human behavior like that which he didn't come to immediately. By 2015, on the anniversary of his capture Ed had been graced with over 70 years to think about it.

He readily admits that he came around to his current attitude in increments. The full extent of Nazi humanity, horrible and grand, became apparent to him ever so slowly, until he could no longer NOT see it. That was when he began to long for something more than condemnation. (Carter-Edwards, 2015)

Finally, he was able to see the full expanse of human capability in the Nazis…the unbelievably horrible capabilities of their lesser angels alongside the breath-taking goodness of their better angels. When one sees the cheery and happy Ed today, with his wife Lowin being loved by their grandchildren, one can't help but wonder if his well-adjusted disposition is due partly to his embracing indiscourageable good will for the Nazis and the people of Weimar, Germany (the village outside Buchenwald Camp). Getting there has been a most beneficial thing, for him and all who know him.

Ferguson, Missouri: One of Many Windows into 21st Century America

As writing commenced on this chapter, a community in Ferguson, Missouri, majority black, policed by minority whites had erupted in pain, rage, burning, looting, militaristic policing and general violence following the shooting death of an unarmed, black youth, Michael Brown, by a white policeman, Darren Wilson. (Wikipedia, 2014) In the days and weeks that followed, evidence emerged that the Civil Rights Acts of the 1960s had been largely withheld and only grudgingly applied in Ferguson. For almost 50 years the black population of Ferguson had been subjected to a perpetual state of covert racism virtually invisible to the outside world.

Stories told by Ferguson residents have since been corroborated by many prominent black leaders from all across the United States who have witnessed the same phenomena in other mixed race communities. Their collective stories are all too numerous of people being pulled over excessively while driving in their own home towns, fined repeatedly and unfairly, searched, abused, injured and humiliated, when no one was looking, simply for being black. Since this story broke in 2014 a new movement has emerged called "Black Lives Matter"…a new mantra for many towns translated as "Love belongs to both White and Black Lives.

Since the summer of 2014, the United States Justice Department investigating the City of Ferguson have reported a history of severe violations of civil rights law. Those who wonder where the indiscourageable good will has gone in places like Ferguson must admit that it was never fully embraced. The task has fallen to a minority of blacks and a few whites who still remember the teachings of the Rev. Dr. Martin Luther King, Jr. 50 years ago.

Occasionally they are the ones heard calling for "calm"…a code word and an echo from the 1960s saying "there is STILL no justification, not even in the 21st century, for responding to injustice with ill-will, no matter who the victims and perpetrators are; no matter what indignities may have been suffered, no matter how many times…no exceptions. To do otherwise only delays justice and everyone's redemption, both black and white.

Looking Ahead As Nations and People Progress From Injustice to Justice

Racism and the legacy of response to it by Rev. Dr. Martin Luther King, Jr., should be allowed to inform our responses to other injustices, whether in Canada, the U.S. or the whole world. It offers a model for responding to (1) the 2016 U.S. Presidential Nomination process, (2) to eliminating poverty, (3) ending terrorism, (4) regulating movement across international boundaries, (5) establishing gender equality, (6) completing progress toward universal health care, (7) maintaining sensible birth control, (8) encouraging wealth distribution, (9) eliminating voter suppression, (10) the influence of wealth on elections, (11) aboriginal relationships, (12) restorative justice in our penal systems, (13) decriminalization of drugs, (14) maintaining religious freedom without restricting the rights of others, (15) obtaining the freedom to die and more. Internationally, indiscourageable good will/the Civil Rights paradigm offer the best guidancc for nations responding to (1) climate change and global warming, (2) the pursuit of alternative sources for global energy, (3) managing the global transition away from carbon-based sources of energy, and (4) managing human resources affected by the transitioning.

Indiscourageable Good Will, the Racial Paradigm & Global Warming

Today as I write there are reports of over 100 drifting glaciers bumping up against the northeast coast of Newfoundland, Canada, having broken loose from ancient moorings in the planet's polar region, because the planet Earth has been warming at an alarming rate, so as usual when things like this happen, the earth-family goes in search of someone to blame. Scientists tell us that humanity is to blame for what's happening now. The accusing finger is pointing at us, yet the people are having difficulty accepting that this can be our fault.

So it's easier to blame energy companies for what's happening because they've been working diligently in high profile way for a 100 years finding and producing the very things which when burned, release carbon gases back into the atmosphere which in turn warm the planet. Once considered global heroes for keeping us warm in winter, cool in summer, providing light at night and power for driving automobiles, they have now become one the world's favorite enemies. While it is true that excessive use of carbon-based energy sources has caused climate problems, it's the people themselves who have driven the search and it is not appropriate nor fair to demonize energy companies who deserve as much indiscourageable good will as anyone in the search for solutions.

Governments, energy companies and the general public, to name just three, will do well to have indiscourageable good will for each other as they move further into the 21st century. Governments must be part of the conversation because they have to provide financial support and enforce regulations; energy companies have to be there because it's their job to find alternative sources of energy; the general public also is needed for providing direction and support. There is no future in vilifying any of these three nor anyone else for what's happened.

So far as carbon-based sources of energy go, there will always be ways for things to go wrong as nations continue using it. Oil spills, blow-outs, water contamination and gas fires are inevitable, so the question is not whether the energy companies can prevent damage to the environment; it's a question of where and when the next spill or contamination or blowout will occur. Even as this chapter was being written, the U.S. Federal Courts had concluded that British Petroleum's blowout in the Gulf of Mexico several months ago was caused partly by "willful neglect by high level employees" with too cozy a relationship between them and government officials. (Davenport, Coral, 2010) (Cozy meaning loss of objectivity and calm.)

It would be better now if energy companies didn't spend a lot of advertising money trying to convince the public that all hydrocarbon development problems have been solved so we can return to business as usual. A better use of money would be spent in appealing to the general public to partner with them in pivoting toward other sources of energy. Governments and people will also do well to remember those energy company employees who will be directly and personally affected by pivoting away from oil, gas, coal. Tax-breaks and subsidies meant to shore up company profits should be reassigned during the interim so that none are abandoned. Indiscourageable good will acknowledges the imperfections of human beings and the institutions they have created; our best option for finding a path through each of the challenges before us.

Extreme Heroism as a Practical, Realistic Way of Life

All the things that can be said about relationships in problem solving, be they interracial, interagency or between governments, corporations, people and environment, can be said about working through every other injustice facing the world. As entertainer Sir Elton John said to those called to Washington, D.C. in 2012 to talk solutions to the AIDS epidemic (Acquired Immune Deficiency Syndrome), "Everyone deserves compassion. Everyone deserves dignity. Everyone, everyone, everyone deserves love."

When he asked rhetorically "Why am I telling you this?" he answered, "Because the Aids disease is caused by a virus, but the Aids epidemic is not. The Aids epidemic is fueled by stigma, violence and indifference," the opposite of good will. (Boseley, 2012) When things don't go well between governments, people, institutions, corporations and others, find the fuel…identify the stigma, expose the violence and the indifference…remove the fuel and then there cannot be such a fire.

Extreme heroism is a way of life that offers a pathway for everyone going through the injustice and that's just about everyone. The rich and the poor don't have to like each other, but they would do well to have indiscourageable good will for each other. In all things the way forward is risky and dangerous yet also practical, sensible and realistic. It is a way of life that has no need to punish but rather provide others with justice.

In his book, "Wishful Thinking" Frederick Buechner wrote, "If we are to love our neighbors, before doing anything else we must see our neighbors. With our imaginations as well as our eyes, that is to say like artists, we must see not just their faces but the life behind and within their faces. Here it is love that is the frame we see them in." (Buechner, 1993)

From his book series entitled "Path of Bliss", the Dalai Lama wrote "The more altruism (extreme heroism) we develop in a day, the more peaceful we find ourselves. Similarly, the more self-centered we remain, the more frustrations and trouble we encounter." (Lama, 2011) Unwavering, steadfast, indiscourageable good will is best learned by doing it and there are plenty of small injustices to practice on. Small successes prepare us for larger successes and we take comfort in the knowledge that human beings were created for this way of life. Take courage also from the knowledge that it is impossible for human beings to hold a hateful thought and good-will in our minds simultaneously.

Law Enforcement and Military Professionals I Have Known

Finally, let me say how grateful I am for the law enforcement and military professionals that I've known over the years, whom I can say were my friends. Those friendly conversations gave me opportunity to speak frankly with them about indiscourageable good will and ask whether or not it's a practical thing to have in their line of work. Does it endanger law enforcement and military professionals or make them safer?

At first thought as they grappled with the question, some said it sounded dangerous but admitted it might not be. One government agent said it did him no good in a drug raid to operate with malice; that malice made it more likely he would make mistakes; that he was more likely to overreact, wound or kill unnecessarily. Indiscourageable good will sounded good to him so long as it didn't mean liking, loving, approving or forgiving right away; it made him a better, safer agent able to deal with more variables.

Indiscourageable good will to him meant levelheadedness and calmness (remember the non-violence advocates in Ferguson, Missouri, calling for calm). My friend told of being on a drug-raid one afternoon, crouched with his squad outside a drug house, poised to break in, when he remembered it was his turn to pick up his son from the day-care center before going home for the evening. It was fast approaching the time when either he or his wife were supposed to be there for their son, so with an AK-47 assault rifle cradled in one arm he reached for his cell-phone and called his wife.

A few seconds later he had averted a domestic crisis and cleared his mind for the professional crisis at hand. The raid was launched, completed, drugs were seized, traffickers arrested and all without death or injury to anyone; no shots were fired. Ideal outcome this time, yes... admittedly, but probably an outcome that can be counted more often than not.

WORKS CITED

Barnard, D. J. (1965). First Christian Church. *Adult Education Class.* Corpus Christi, Texas, USA.

Boseley, S. (2012, July 24). International AIDS Conference Washington, D.C. *The Guardian.*

Buechner, F. (1993). *Wishful Thinking.* San Francisco: HarperOne.

Carter-Edwards, E. (2015, May 4). Canadian Vet Revisits Buchenwald on VE Day 2015. (C. T. National, & B. Scheerer, Interviewers)

Davenport, Coral. (2010, August). *New York Times.* Retrieved May 4, 2015, from nytimes.com: www.nytimes.com

King, J. M. (1965). *Sojourners.* Retrieved September 18, 2006, from Verse & Voice: www.sojo.net

Lama, D. (2011). *Sojourners.* Retrieved June 1, 2011, from Verse & Voice: www.sojo.net

Spielberg, S. (Director). (1985). *The Color Purple* [Motion Picture].

Wikipedia. (2014, August). Retrieved May 2, 2015, from www.wikipedia.org: en.wikipedia.org

EPILOGUE - EXTREME HEROISM

Extreme Heroism: Foolproof or Fool's Errand;
Safe, Risky, Downright Dangerous

How about all the above? Foolproof: It truly is a way through the injustices of life like no other. Fool's errand: Sometimes justice is incredibly elusive, giving the impression of no progress. Safe: Often, yet Risky: Always, at some level. Never without disturbance. Downright dangerous: Sometimes. Just so you know.

Christians call this danger the cost of discipleship, the way of Jesus or the cost of learning. Without doubt other religious folk have names for it too. Non-religious have my permission to call it extreme heroism until they believe they have something better to call it.

In 1995, song-writer Gordon Light (Light, 2007) published a song entitled "*My Love Colours Outside the Lines*" whose lyrics declare "We'll never move the gravestones if we're not prepared to die and realize, there are worlds outside the lines." With these bold words he proclaims to Christians the solemn truth about *the way of Jesus* that is also true for extreme heroes, people of the inner light or those simply seeking balance in their life. It's a free gift to all...one with many names...whether we're child heroes, adult heroes or elder heroes.

Whether speaking boldly, singing boldly or acting boldly, extreme heroes must realize they are pushing the boundaries, creating disturbances in many worlds as they try to move toward justice. No one knows in advance in setting out to embrace the concept of extreme heroism whether their actions will actually serve justice or simply add to the injustice. The stories of extreme heroism shared so far in this book are mostly success stories which is fair because most stories of extreme heroism have good consequences whether we respond to an injustice by legal means, prophetic words or parabolic teaching; artistic expression or whistle-blowing or some other creative response, but extreme heroes must be realistic about the fine line they walk between justice and injustice, liberation and persecution, truth and slander. It is incredibly important at all times that extreme heroes remain humble and on the alert.

No one wants to accidently cross over to the dark side, but it can happen. First choices in responding to injustice can be seductive and wrong. Second and third choices must be weighed carefully, but sometimes there's no time for careful sifting of options. Heroes encounter intense support at times for keeping things unchanged.

No one knows the magnitude of the injustice they may one day be facing or the magnitude of the risks they might have to take. There's only one thing worse however, than accidentally making a mistake: it's doing nothing, not even praying.

Creative Extremists of Dr. King and Extreme Heroes

You can understand why I found great comfort in coming to the final stages of writing this book, *Extreme Heroism*, to discover the following quotation by Rev. Dr. Martin Luther King, Jr. in which he himself uses the word extremist and in a good way. In a published sermon he wrote: "The question is not whether we will be extremists, but what kind of extremists we will be…The nation and the world are in dire need of creative extremists." (King, 1965) Thank you Dr. King for saying so. It is as important that we be creative extremists as it is to avoid destructive extremism.

Everyone knows of course that Dr. King and other Civil Rights Advocates were living, breathing examples of creative extremism and if I may say so, extreme heroes. While I do not know whether Dr. King ever used the words extreme and heroism in the same sentence, I consider it a safe bet that we are talking about the same things. The better part of heroism is extreme and creatively so, which brings us to two more stories of extreme heroism (which can also be called creative extremism).

In each of the following stories there will be reminders of our two natures…what some call "our better angels" versus "lesser angels". The fact is that everyone, until they are fully aware of themselves, move easily from one set of angels to the other set and then back again. Ideally, as human beings mature, they take a stand more and more often with their better side in the face of injustice.

Some adults, however, never mature; that is, they never take a stand with their better angels. Like many politicians, who waffle back and forth from one side or the other, they choose to live perpetually with all their options open as if their better angels and lesser angels were equal. It is inevitable then that bad choices will be made when faced with severe and emergent injustice, but remember that just thinking about doing violence in itself does not disqualify any from extreme heroism.

The first story comes out of Nazi Germany in the 1940s at the height of World War II; the second is a story from the 1960s in peace-time Canada.

The Reverend Dietrich Bonhoeffer – German Lutheran Theologian

The name Dietrich Bonhoeffer, Lutheran Clergyperson, is a name known to Christians everywhere with any significant history with the larger Church (Wikipedia, 2016). His name and his story come up at some point in every seminary education, whether for Catholic Priests or a Protestant Ministers. He was one of many clergy who came to the point of responding to Adolf Hitler and the Nazi injustices of World War II, by giving thought to Hitler's assassination.

Actually coming to that point and seizing upon it would have been difficult for anyone, because so many were flocking to Hitler with adoration, but his choices must have been even more difficult as one steeped in the values of indiscourageable good will, love, grace and forgiveness. However, within two days of Hitler's election as Germany's Chancellor, Bonhoeffer began pushing back against Hitler's announced policies...with prophetic words. In radio addresses he began warning the German people of the danger he saw in what they had just done at the ballot box, electing Hitler as Chancellor.

It wasn't long before the Gestapo banned his radio broadcasts, but Bonhoeffer would find other ways to continue his campaign of words against Hitler, speaking as often as he could to churches and other organizations. The Gestapo patiently pursued him and responded to what he was saying by further and further restrictions on his public speaking. Then, when the Gestapo learned that other German clergy were considering Hitler's assassination, Bonhoeffer was linked to them and their presumed plot.

Suspected of collaborating, Bonhoeffer was arrested. He spent the rest of his life in prison, writing to the church...sharing his learnings with everyone who could read. He was executed by the Nazis when Allied forces seemed destined to win the war.

Chief Blackwater...Gitxsan First Nation

Turning to the second story, the name Willie Blackwater, is becoming a name known to many Canadians who care about the Truth and Reconciliation Conferences of 1998-2015 which were part of a national response to the injustices against Canada's aboriginal people that began coming to light in the 1960s. The source of that injustice was The Canadian Indian Residential School System (schools similar to schools in the United States known as The American Indian Boarding Schools). (Wikipedia, 2016) In both countries the schools were designed for assimilating aboriginal children into the dominant European culture which had colonized North America after the 1600s.

Chief Blackwater, as he's now known, is being hailed as a hero (Wright, Fighter, The, 2016) for his youthful response to injustices against him and other aboriginal children. The greater injustice of course had been the ripping of aboriginal children from their relationships with families, native language, culture and the land which then led to separating many of the children from their own sexual identity. It has now been argued that the governments and churches of Canada and U.S. were merely responding to the injustice which they perceived had been created by language and cultural disparities.

Meaning well in what they were doing, only masked the injustice they were compounding. The European attitudes which prevailed toward native people is disturbing to even think about in 2016. The words arrogant and contemptuous barely capture their perceptions.

At the very earliest beginning of their plans to assimilate, there were leaders like Henry Knox in the United States who lamented the real intentions of the two governments and national churches. As the first Secretary of War for the U.S., Knox wrote to President, George Washington, saying "I suspect [their plan] was more convenient than just." (Wikipedia, 2016) He further mused to Washington how different things might be if instead of assimilation they had set out to educate aboriginal children and their adults. In all probability there would have been some who could see the possibility of aboriginal people teaching the colonists, but that was not to be. One wonders nowadays, given the condition of our planet's environment today, what might have been learned back then about relationships with the Earth, if that generation had been willing to be learn from aboriginal people.

Assimilation in both countries proved terribly violent at every invisible level…emotional, intellectual and spiritual. The violence in Canada remained hidden until it began to surface in the 1960s as widespread sexual abuse against the children became apparent. This is where Chief Blackwater, then known by his English name, Willie, came into the picture.

He was a 13-year-old boy by then, all but swallowed up by the system before he martialed his strength for pushing back against sexual injustice. Sexual injustice wasn't limited to the Roman Catholic Church by any means. It was in the midst of a sexual incident, that Willie realized he could take no more, resolving the next time it happened to be armed with a razor sharp kitchen knife.

In turning on his abuser and putting the knife to the man's throat, Willie did not foreclose on the man's life, but he did present him with options…an end to the sexual abuse for Willie or the possibility of death, right then and there. The risk to Willie in this dramatic moment must not be trivialized. While it clearly endangered the life of his abuser in that moment, it also endangered Willie in the very instant that he withdrew the knife.

Please be aware of the good will he must have had at some level for his abuser before dwelling too long on the obvious implications of ill will. The risk for Willie must have gone through the roof in the moments after he removed the knife. He would have to trust that his abuser would do the right thing and not retaliate. Perhaps it was residual goodness in the abuser that kicked in after that leading him to keep his word. The abuse toward Willie stopped.

This act of extreme heroism came breathtakingly close to going wrong until it went right. It affords us with opportunity to see the connectedness of the emotional, spiritual, mental and physical death. One is never far from the others, whether we're a teenager Willie, or a teenager sharing loose change with someone else's child at the Dollar Store (Ch. 5), or we're a reporter with the Washington Post receiving intelligence from Deep Throat (Ch. 13.

Even simple acts of befriending can endanger; simple acts of inclusion, sharing, can too. So there must always be some degree of awareness about us that in doing good we might encounter someone's lesser angels. Blackwater's resistance to injustice was not simple nor without great danger…never guaranteed to bring about the change desired…perhaps opening a door to greater abuse.

On the better side of things, Blackwater's heroism set in motion a series of semi-legal responses that resulted in something like a class-action lawsuit – namely, a national conversation with the nation and the church who listened to the 14,000 victims that had been created by the system. Neither Government nor Church had seen their attitudes toward aboriginal people as a source of the problem until it was too late. Yet not too late because those cases together have brought into the light a foundation for a new and encouraging chapter in First Nations-Canadian relationships.

Dietrich Bonhoeffer and Chief Blackwater were moved by the circumstances of their situations to go where no one desires to go… threatening or challenging the well-being of those involved in wrong-doing. Neither Bonhoeffer nor Blackwater actually pulled the trigger or thrust the knife so to speak, but the options for doing so were clearly on the table. Bonhoeffer has been declared a hero posthumously without his actions being identified with heroism; Blackwater has been unabashedly declared a hero by many, including RCMP Officer Al Franczak and by Lawyer Peter Grant, according to Richard Wright's article (Wright, The Fighter, 2016) in The Observer magazine.

Not everyone however, is faced with responding to the kinds of injustice which faced Bonhoeffer and Blackwater. Not every injustice threatens immediate harm to humanity but every injustice, however small, is the first step in a whole series of big steps which deserve to be pushed back against.

Heroes David Thompson-English Immigrant; Charlotte Small-Cree Nation

Extreme heroes (creative extremists) have emerged in every generation, but don't let the word extreme or extremist fool you. The words are not meant to mean brash or noticeable, but maybe just the opposite of such terms. Extreme and extremist is less about attention getting and more about its effectiveness, importance and value.

The result of this is that extreme heroes briefly capture the attention of those in the immediate vicinity of a heroic act; in other words, the recipients…the beneficiaries…who can often be just one person. The memories of one and the memories of many are about the same length before the persons doing the heroic things are all but forgotten. While the benefits of their heroism linger on, perhaps forever, extreme heroism does not usually get the kind of attention that was given Bonhoeffer and Blackwater because the beneficiaries of extreme heroism usually take their good fortune for granted, seldom giving any thought as to why their lives are noticeably improved.

The names of many, many extreme heroes/creative extremists… women, children, elder adults and men…have been forgotten...simply because their contributions were not sufficiently spectacular. In 2009, journalist John Allemang joined several people trying to correct this sad fact about a map-maker from the late 1700s and early 1800s, named David Thompson, by writing an article for The Globe & Mail entitled, "In Praise of David Thompson." In that article Allemang mentions two authorities on the subject, William E. Moreau, a Toronto teacher and researcher, and Don Gillmor, author of the book *Kanata*, but it was Allemang who said in so many words that it was well past time for Canadians to show some love for David Thompson as a Canadian hero.

In his own careful qualifying of the word hero, Allemang comes close to defining David as an extreme hero, saying…"not by being a hero in the romantic way, nor in the sense of being a rugged individual who struck out on his own through perilous lands and warring savages, but as someone who worked his way slowly, methodically in co-operation with native people on behalf of his employer, a fur-trading company. If he wasn't heroic according to the traditional paradigm, he was heroic in his vision [a very apt description of an extreme hero or creative extremist], open-minded, observant and methodical; as Canadian heroes go, that will do quite nicely for now". (Allemang, 2009).

Parks Canada in a report (Brown, 2007-2013) goes on to paint a picture of David Thompson as incomplete without also picturing his wife, Charlotte Small. If David was an extreme hero then so was Charlotte. They were together too long, accomplishing too much and enduring far too much for it to be otherwise.

Born to her Cree mother and her Scottish-born father, Charlotte was an indispensable partner, provider, spokesperson, companion and a master of the Cree and English languages which she used to pave the way for David in his relationships with tribal leaders. His success or failure in map-making, not to mention survival in the wilderness, depended on her. Unlike Charlotte's Scottish father and other explorer-fur traders from Europe, who fathered children with Cree women and then left them stranded at some frontier outpost, Thompson was loyal to Charlotte, making her his wife on June 10, 1799, according to Cree law and custom.

Charlotte returned David's gesture with one of her own, thirty years later when the couple moved with their children to Montreal and married again according to Presbyterian law and custom. Thompson wrote about Charlotte in his mapping and travel journals calling her his "lovely wife" and praising her for her survival skills in the wilderness, which helped keep them fed. Her language skills David wrote, "…gives me a great advantage." (Brown, 2007-2013)

Evidence shows that David and Charlotte shared a mutual respect for people, their knowledge and customs, which in itself is extreme heroism. They had respect also for the animals, forests, water-ways and mountains; that also is extreme. Thompson wrote in his journals of setting aside his own biases with regard to aboriginal understanding of the mass migration of caribou saying he could no longer fall back on European explanations of animal instinct, but instead he learned to favor the concept of "higher orders from the Great Manitou".

Charlotte was 13 years old when they married and David was 29, but in spite of the sixteen years between them when David died in 1857, Charlotte died just three months later. Allemang was right to call David a "new kind of hero" but we would be doing Charlotte a great disservice to overlook the depth to which she was David's soul-mate. If one of them was an extreme hero, then both were. His maps and their mutually respectful relationships with the people and the land set the stage…paved the way…for a different and better Canada for those who followed.

John Smith & Pocahontas; Lewis, Clark & Sacajawea – Heroes Maybe

The United States has had its share of people, male and female, who I'm sure were cut from the same cloth as Thompson and Small, but apparently there's a lack of written evidence for that; at least that's what

I've been told. Unlike Thompson who kept meticulous records of his work, travels and life with Charlotte, there was no similar evidence from relationships between Captain John Smith and Algonquin native Pocahontas from the 1600s on the northeast coast U.S. nor between explorers out west in the 1800s, Lewis, Clark and Shoshone native Sacajawea. This is particularly interesting to me since growing up in Wyoming, the home of the Shoshone Tribe, I was fed stories in grade school about Sacajawea's warm and supportive relationship.

If in truth there is no factual evidence to support these heroic notions then at least someone wanted that to be true and saw no problem with telling such stories to my generation. While these stories may not be factual, it's hard to imagine how any nation could be successful without people behaving this way…as extreme heroes do, whether female or male. No nation would have come as far as the U.S. and Canada have without such people, but it would not be the first time in history that men failed to notice and mention female heroes who were with them, supporting them, nor would it be the first time that relationship makers were taken for granted and promptly forgotten.

Lawrence Hill in his book, "Blood: The Stuff of Life" (Hill, 2013), that inspired the television series, "The Book of Negroes", tells of a childhood incident in which he was injured, cut, bleeding and rushing home to get his mother's help. He remembers the vividness of the red colored blood as it splashed onto the sidewalk all the way home and then its dullness later after only a couple of days, turning brown and rust-colored until it disappeared altogether along with everyone's memory of whose blood that happened to be, not to mention the dramatic story that went with it…swallowed up in just a few days as though it had ever happened.

So it is with much of the extreme heroism and creative extremism which has come before us. Its vivid colors for those who saw it happen and equally vivid memories of those whose heroism produced such dramatic stories, are always vulnerable to disappearing again without so much as a trace, unless there's someone around who knows how important such events and stories are, to all subsequent generations. It is partly the responsibility of those who were there and then those who knew those who were there and were willing to keep the stories alive for future generations.

It is the "blood" of extreme heroism/creative extremism that still flows behind all of our remembrances in Canada and the United States... Remembrance Day, Memorial Day and Veterans Day...lest we forget... because we will forget about the heroism unless we take steps to make sure we don't. It was Bernard Malamud (Malamud, 1952), a Jewish American author who wrote of a mystery he called natural heroism. He used a fictional baseball player named Roy Hobbs in his book, "The Natural" (which was made into a movie starring Robert Redford), to declare: "Without heroes we are all plain people, and don't know how far we can go." We ourselves are forgetful of our own heroism.

Let us correct the mistakes of our forebears by being resolved henceforth to recognize and honor every day someone's extreme heroism in all things and in all people...family, church, mosque, synagogue, school, work, and neighborhood. There are more than enough extreme heroes in our community, nation and the world; what's missing is our consciousness of them and our lips, writings and actions giving them the acclaim they deserve.

* * *

Extreme Heroes, Creative Extremists, Altruistic, Justice-Minded, Saintly, Holy, Priestly, Honoring, Respecting, Enlightened, Good Will Indiscourageable, Steadfast, Everlasting, Hard-Wired, Ambassadors, Diplomats, Peace-makers, Inclusive, Domain of Children, Domain of Elders, Domain of Women, Domain of Men, Domain of Any Sexual Orientation, Domain of All Races, Domain of the Poor & Disadvantaged, Domain of the Under- Privileged

(Picture a "wordle" combining these words to show extreme heroism's universalism and powerful function.)

WORKS CITED

Allemang, J. (2009, September 19). *Globe and Mail Toronto*, p. F4.(Permission to use from Globe & Mail Editor Sylvia Stead, 23March2016)

Brown, J. S. (2007-2013). *Charlotte Small, Person of National Historic Significance.* Parks Canada.

Centre, C. N. (2010). Truth and Reconciliation Conferences. Winnipeg, Manitoba, Canada.

Hill, L. (2013). *Blood: The Stuff of Life.* Toronto: House of Anansi Press.

King, J. M. (1965). *Sojourners.* Retrieved September 18, 2006, from Verse & Voice: www.sojo.net

Light, G. (2007). My Love Colours Outside The Lines. In U. C. Canada, *More Voices* (p. 138). Toronto: United Church Publishing House.

Malamud, B. (1952). *Natural, The.* New York: Farrar, Straus & Cudahy.

Wikipedia. (2016, March 12). Retrieved from www://en.Wikipedia.org/wiki/American_Indian_Boarding_Schools and Canadian Indian Residential School System.

Wright, R. (2016, March). The Fighter. *United Church Observer, The*, pp. 30-36.

ACKNOWLEDGMENTS

From a whole life of being among extreme heroes...sometimes knowing it...sometimes, not...many of them not knowing they were heroes either...but now...I know...

Thanks to my birth family that included extreme heroes like my mother and father, Edna and Joe; my brothers Harry, Barry and sister-in-law Connie; my grandparents Eugene and Edith...Joseph and Anna; my cousins Judy Hauff and Chuck Prochaska.

Thanks to my early childhood classmates who were standout extreme heroes...especially Eddie and Rita. Thanks to my middle-grade and high school teachers Nell Pate, Mary Nichols, Kathleen Hemry, Daniel Deti, Milton Beitel. Thanks to my high school classmates Gene Prugh, Jerry Goodnight, Mickey McGrath, Dugan Simmons, Gale Peterson, Peggy Doll, Georgia Doll, Betty Jean Alexander, Mary Louise Whiffen; my college and university friends including Sally Force, Jon Helzer, Chuck Claver; teachers Don Boyd and Senator Gale McGee; and my youth ministers, including Charles Rose and The Reverend Jack V. Reeve.

Thanks to my military friends, including Sid Caperton.

Thanks to my first marriage family including Betty, our children Mike, Gena and Jay; my first in-laws... Isaac and Georgia Leach, Raymond Leach.

Thanks to my first church as an adult layman, Corpus Christi, Texas; senior minister Oliver W. Harrison; church leaders like Jimmy Barnard, Charlie Palmer, Vaughn Bowen, Clarence and Joan Smith

Thanks to my energy-seeking/finding friends and mentors at Atlantic Refining Company, Atlantic Richfield, Southern Union Gas Company and Burns Petroleum; Joe Coester, Bob Agatston, Bob McGinnis, Walt Baker, Joe Birchum, Walt Steiner, Tony, Larry Ley.

Thanks to heroes of my second adult church, Northway Christian Church, Dallas, Texas; it's senior minister Patrick Henry, Jr; Oran and Charlotte Nabors.

Thanks to the chaplain and acquaintances in 1969 at Huntsville Federal Prison, Texas.

Thanks to my beloved seminary friends like Dennis and Dianne of Brite Divinity School, Ft. Worth, Texas.

Thanks to my seminary teachers and standout extreme heroes Dick Hoehn, George Smith, Charles Kemp, Marcus Bryant, Glenn Routt, John Stewart, Jack Suggs, Bill Hall and William Tucker. Thanks to Carl and Stephanie Simonton.

Thanks to all the heroes of the Northwest Region (Auburn, Washington) including Laura Bethards; Melanie Raymond; the Southwest Region (Kaufman, Texas) and the South Central Conference (San Antonio, Kurten, Richland Hills, and The Woodlands, Texas); including heroes like Bill Goodykoontz, Deb Hart, Paul and Pauline Stone; the Alberta and B.C. Conferences (Calgary, Alberta; Burnaby, B.C); the Nebraska Conference (Lincoln, Sutton, Falls City) including Kenneth Moore, George Worcester, Bob Loffer; the Rocky Mountain Conference (Casper, Wheatland, Gillette, Newcastle, Rock Springs, Laramie and Douglas, Wyoming) including Vern and Tami Moore, Dawn Sorg, Dave and LeAnn Thompson, Vickie Tillard, Trina McDaniel, Vickie and Sissy Goodwin.

Thanks to the heroes at Campbell-Stone United Church, St. Andrews United Church, Wesley United Church, The Pastoral Institute of Calgary including Gordon and Kay Bandola, Todd Nakamura, Jack and Alice Baldwin, Jim and Mary Henderson, David and Pat Lovewell,

Betty Cameron, Ralph Milton, Bev and Ron Coates, Fausta Milan, Ed and Kay Mullen.

Thanks to Carol my partner in professional ministry and marriage for over 33 years and her children Lonnie and Dena who became part of our blending family, my second set of in-laws Eileen and Bill Partin; Tom and Laurie Magnuson.

Thanks to the budding heroes in my grandchildren: Rhys, Kavan, Hailey, Jordan, Isaac, Amelia, Parker, Emiko and Zane; son's-in-law Mark and Roland; daughters-in-law Kirsten and Nicole.

Thanks to those who have been a source of support and encouragement in the latter stages of writing this book…Verna Relkoff, John and Ali Galm, Tamara Abramson, Judy Cameron, Donna Strongman, Peter Busby, David Boyd, Nolan Gingrich, Trish Morrison and the Lenten Study Group of 2014 that included Doug Scott at Nelson United Church.

Thanks to those many heroes whose names have slipped from my mental grasp but whose faces and heroic acts remain etched in my memory; thanks to those heroes whom I never knew at the time were acting heroically, especially those who responded to me out of the goodness of their own hearts when I, a stranger, needed support. And thanks be to the one who created us all to be extreme heroes. Sincerely, John Prochaska

"I am large, I contain multitudes." – Walt Whitman

CPSIA information can be obtained
at www.ICGtesting.com
Printed in the USA
FSOW01n2249281216
28993FS